Historic Landscapes Summit County, Colorado Railroad Stations and Sites
Volume 1
Boreas Pass, Farnham, and More

By
Bill Fountain
Sandra Mather, PhD

Copyright © 2024 Summit Historical Society

All Rights Reserved. No portion of this book may be reproduced in any form or by any electronic or mechanical means, including information storage and retrieval systems, without permission from the publisher, except by a reviewer who may quote brief passages in review.

Published in the United States of America by Summit Historical Society Press,
103 LaBonte Street, P.O. Box 143, Dillon, Colorado 80435

www.summithistorical.org

Historic Landscapes, Summit County, Colorado,
Railroad Stations and Sites,
Volume 1: Boreas Pass, Farnham, and More

Authors: Bill Fountain and Sandra F. Mather, PhD
Editors: Bill Fountain and Sandra F. Mather, PhD

1st edition date: November 1, 2024

ISBN: 978-1-943829-64-4

Library of Congress Control Number: 2024948862

Summit Historical Society Press is an imprint of Rhyolite Press LLC,
P.O. Box 60144, Colorado Springs, CO 80960.

This book is sponsored by Richard Yount.

Cover Photos:
Top: Engine No. 113 at Rocky Point

Bottom trio L to R:
Eastbound Colorado & Southern Train taking on Water at Bakers Tank, 1935
Train at Farnham Station heading toward Boreas Pass, 1884
Westbound Train passing Eastbound Train on Siding at Argentine/Bacon, 1920

Book Design & Layout: Marla Morelos

Table of Contents

Acknowledgements 4

Prologue 5

Chapter 1 7
Overview of Railroads in Summit County

Chapter 2 41
Boreas Pass Station

Chapter 3 75
Farnham Station

Chapter 4 89
Farnham Spur

Chapter 5 111
Dwyer/Belmont Station

Chapter 6 127
Signature Sandstone

Chapter 7 133
Bakers Tank

Chapter 8 173
Argentine/Bacon Station

Chapter 9 211
Rocky Point

Bibliography 224

Index 226

About the Authors 228

Acknowledgements

As with any publication, certain individuals, governmental agencies, and other entities provided vital assistance, support, and encouragement. A big thank you goes to Maureen Nicholls, Robin Theobald, Ed and Nancy (deceased) Bathke, Rich Skovlin, Rick Hague, Larissa O'Neil, Kris Ann Knish, Robert Phillippi, Kurt Maechner, *Colorado Postal Historian*, the Breckenridge History Archives, the Summit Historical Society, History Colorado, Summit County Clerk and Recorder's Office, and the Bureau of Land Management in Lakewood, Colorado.

Much of the research comes from the Colorado Historic Newspaper Collection website (www.coloradohistoricnewspapers.org). *The Summit County Journal*, the *Breckenridge Bulletin*, and the *Summit County Journal and Breckenridge Bulletin* (The two merged for almost five years beginning in October, 1909.) are available online from 1892 until early 1923.

M.C. Poor's book, *Denver South Park & Pacific*, provided preliminary information about railroad stations and stops. Although it continues to be a valuable resource, authors have identified inconsistencies and inaccuracies in that publication. It must be remembered that Poor conducted his research before the internet.

We send a special thank you to Jerry Eggleston for allowing us to use postcards and postmarked envelopes from his collection.

We extend heartfelt gratitude to Eric Twitty, owner of Mountain States Historical, for granting us special permission to quote and use maps from his Colorado Cultural Resource Survey. His research and writing truly enhanced the quality of our manuscript.

Extensive support came from Bob Schoppe, president of the Denver, South Park & Pacific Historical Society. Bob provided maps and photographs from the Society's collection and shared his vast knowledge of the narrow-gauge railroads of Summit County.

The aerial photographs at the end of the chapters came from Google Earth.

A very special thank you to Mike Shipley, CEO of Key Media, who offered the services of his company in laying out not only this book but all seven in this series. Mike owns the Country Boy Mine in French Gulch near Breckenridge, which draws tourists and residents alike to experience an authentic late 1800s mine. Mike also supported the publication of the book, *Country Boy Mine, Breckenridge, Colorado, 1881 – 1994*, by Fountain and Mather.

Also, many thanks to Marla Morelos, Head of Graphic Design for Key Media, for preparing the layout. She has become a treasured colleague.

Prologue

Why *Historic Landscapes, Railroad Stations and Sites of Summit County, Colorado*? Bill Fountain explains: My idea of writing a book about the long-vanished railroad stops of Summit County arose while I planned the first five volumes of the *Historic Landscapes* series that focused on the historic towns of Summit County found from Hoosier Pass north to the confluence of the Blue and Swan rivers and from the Ten Mile Range east to the historic towns of Rexford and Swandyke. As I started identifying the historic sites within my chosen boundaries, I decided to include railroad stations, even though some of them were not truly townsites. I selected 26 sites—some relatively unknown; some known by a few. About most, little had been written.

Using information that I had gathered from first-hand accounts, Denver, South Park & Pacific files, public archives, newspaper articles written by those who had observed and reported what they saw, and the hundreds of photographs in my files available to tell the interesting stories of the sites, I found many important stories that had not been told before, deserving of two volumes devoted entirely to the railroad sites. I, alone and with others, explored the sites, mentally traveling back in time, imagining life at those locations over 150 years ago. I hope readers will do the same as they read the books in this series.

Figure PR-1 includes the location of all the ghost towns, historic townsites, and train stations found in *Historic Landscapes, Summit County, Colorado*.

Financial difficulties led to changes in ownership over the years. The Denver, South Park, founded in 1873, became the Denver, Leadville & Gunnison in 1889 only to be sold to the Colorado & Southern in 1899.

    1873-1889 – Denver, South Park & Pacific
    1889-1899 Denver, Leadville & Gunnison
    1899-1937 Colorado & Southern
    (The Chicago, Burlington & Quincy purchased the Colorado & Southern in 1906 and kept the corporate name on its standard-gauge operations until 1982.)

Sidings and spurs played important roles. Although both refer to tracks leading off the main line, they had different functions. A siding, with a switch at each end, allowed a train to leave the main line so another could pass through. A spur had only one switch. A train on a spur had to back out to return to the main line.

Historic Landscapes, Summit County, Colorado Railroad Stations and Sites Volume 1

Figure PR-1. Map of a Portion of Summit County showing Ghost Towns, Historic Townsites, and Train Stations.

CHAPTER 1
NARROW-GAUGE RAILROADS IN SUMMIT COUNTY

Two Narrow-Gauge Railroads

The development of the mining and agricultural economies of Summit County required cheap, efficient transportation. From the spring of 1859 on, when prospectors discovered gold in what became Summit County, adequate, reliable transportation meant the difference between economic advantage and stagnation. Without it, ore, hay, timber, sheep, and cattle could not reach local or distant markets; food, clothing, and mining and agricultural equipment and supplies would not be available for those needing them.

Although pack trains and wagons carried a staggering tonnage of merchandise and ore to and from Summit County, some pieces of equipment for the mines proved far too heavy and bulky to be carried by wagon and sled. Stockpiled ore had to be moved more quickly and at cheaper rates to be profitable. Merchants and miners required something that could carry larger loads faster and at less expense—that something was the railroad.

Two narrow-gauge railroads served Summit County: The Denver Rio Grande Western and the Denver, South Park & Pacific. The word "Pacific" told of the company's desire to reach the Pacific Ocean. Investors and entrepreneurs created both as a means of efficiently moving the mineral wealth of the county, thus tying their fortunes to the mining economy. When it died, so too did the railroads.

The president of the Denver & Rio Grande, William Jackson Palmer, felt that "a population engaged in mining is by far the most profitable of any for a railroad." Therefore, he built the Leadville, Ten Mile & Breckenridge Railroad (officially the Leadville & Ten Mile Narrow Gauge Railroad), which ran from Leadville through the Ten Mile Canyon, serving Robinson and Kokomo by December, 1880; Wheeler [Copper Mountain] by September, 1881; and Dillon by November, 1882, a distance of 36 miles.

A plan that never materialized included a route to Kremmling that would have tapped the ranches lining the lower Blue River. A March 23, 1881, article gushed with excitement:

> "Promises of Railroads Cheered the Growing Mining District,
> Then Entirely Dependent Upon Crude Means for Transportation and Freight
> Last evening we were called upon by Mr. E. L. Jones of Golden, who was

here . . . to employ a large number of men and proceed to break ground at once. The superintendent, Mr. Jones, is not the man to allow grass to grow under his feet. The workmen were engaged last night, and will go to work tomorrow morning. The road was surveyed two years ago, but for want of confidence work was not commenced, but now they propose making up for lost time, and will grade the roadbed down the Blue by way of Dillon, in the Grand and Hot Sulphur Springs, thence to North Park, and eventually to Laramie . . . The superintendent will set at work at once as many graders and tie cutters as he can employ. This looks like business and we expect to see the iron horse in the valley of the Blue ere another fall's snows cover the ground." (*Daily Journal*)

Rumors flew again in May, 1902, that the Denver & Rio Grande would finally build its extension north. The railroad graded along the waterway as far as Green Mountain and laid track about a mile north of Dillon. A train ran over the short extension each day to maintain the right-of-way. Eventually even this stopped. After workers removed the rails and ties, the grade became a county road.

The Denver, South Park & Pacific (DSP&P), created by Gov. John Evans in 1872, became part of the Union Pacific rail system in 1880. Led by Jay Gould, the railroad wanted its own line to Leadville rather than share one as it had been doing with the Denver & Rio Grande. Railroad surveyors arrived in the county in June, 1881. Feeling that the county's mineral resources, especially in the Snake River valley, warranted its attention, the railroad decided to begin work at once on a main line that would fully control passenger and freight service in the county. The company planned to build spurs to mines off the main track. The newspaper editor crowed that with the coming of the railroad, Breckenridge would "be lifted into the list of cities within the pale of civilization. It [Breckenridge] would have distribution facilities almost equal to Denver."

The railroad planned to enter the county from two directions. From the north, the Georgetown, Breckenridge and Leadville Railroad would extend its Clear Creek line over Loveland Pass and follow the Snake to its confluence with the Blue River in Dillon. Branches would then be built to Breckenridge and Leadville. From the south, the railroad would enter Summit County from South Park using one of three routes: over Georgia Pass and down French Gulch to Breckenridge; over Boreas Pass and down Indiana Creek to Illinois Gulch and Breckenridge; or over Hoosier Pass and down the Blue valley to Breckenridge. Whichever route the railroad chose, Leadville, not Breckenridge, was the primary destination. Based on their surveys, the railroad chose Breckenridge Pass, in 1882 renamed Boreas Pass, which was 21 miles shorter, lower in elevation, and made use of an already-graded wagon road.

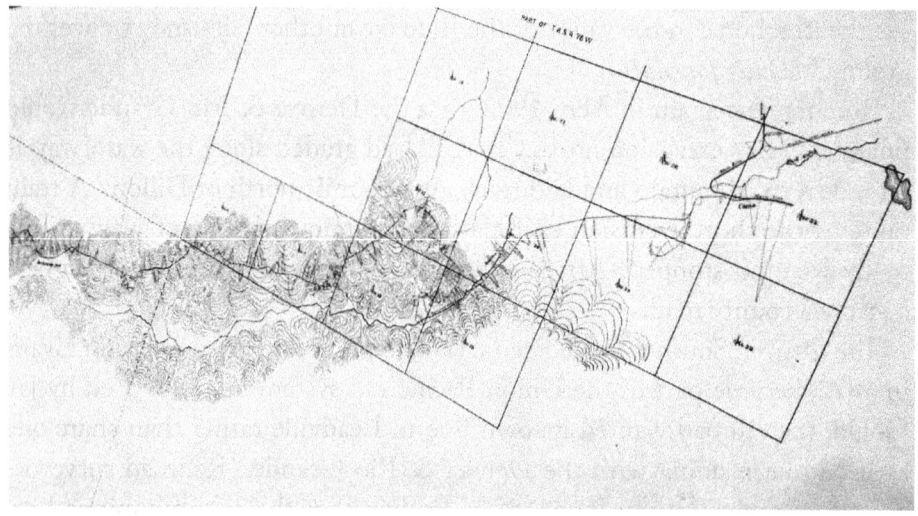

Figure 1-1. Portion of a DSP&P Map showing the Surveyed Route from Como in South Park to Breckenridge Pass, 1880. The railroad changed the name of Breckenridge Pass to Boreas Pass in 1881. (Courtesy Bob Schoppe)

From Como

The railroad began laying track in Como in 1881, reaching Breckenridge Pass (Boreas Pass) by the end of the year. The tracks extended to Breckenridge by September, 1882, and Dillon by December, 1882. The line continued through the Ten Mile Canyon, arriving in Leadville in 1884.

The original Denver, South Park survey called for the line from Breckenridge to meet a line from the east at Dillon. By revising the plans so that the lines met at Dickey (also called Placer Junction), two miles south of Dillon, the company saved four miles of track and shortened the distance to Leadville.

The company proposed an extension to tap the mines of the Montezuma and Chihuahua districts, cross Loveland Pass from the west, and connect with the Georgetown line. Crews laid the seven miles of track from Dillon to Keystone by January, 1883. The people of Montezuma, as well as those in Chihuahua and Decatur in the Peru Creek valley, began an active campaign to get the attention of the railroad. Newspapers "boosted" the area; mining companies and individuals cajoled, petitioned, and threatened; officials of the line accepted invitations to visit and see the potential for profit. Despite vociferous urging by the miners, the tracks never extended beyond Keystone. The railroad felt that the mines did not produce enough ore to make the plan financially sound even though their earlier assessment indicated otherwise.

Damn Slow Pulling and Pretty Rough Riding

The mountain railroads of Colorado laid their rails three feet apart. Railroads in the East and on the plains used standard gauge, meaning four feet, eight and one-half inches between the rails. Narrow-gauge tracks offered advantages. Sharp turns so necessary in the mountains required less blasting. It proved cheaper to go around objects rather than through them. The shorter ties saved money, as did the smaller, lighter engines and cars. Narrow-gauge track could be laid faster. Rather than cut and grade new beds, the railroads bought rights-of-way from wagon companies. Crews laid iron rails on untreated ties of spruce and yellow pine spaced 18 inches apart, using approximately 3,000 ties per mile. Rocks blasted from the bed and, later, cinders from passing engines become ballast. Ashes from the firebox, dumped along the tracks, added to the ballast. Work crews did little true grading as the companies rushed to complete their lines. Tracks bent and sagged in the middle, causing the cars to sway sideways and lurch forward and backward. Maximum speeds for passenger trains reached less than 22 miles per hour in the county and less that 12 miles per hour for freight trains in the Ten Mile Canyon and over Boreas Pass. Passengers did not enjoy a speedy, comfortable ride. Instead, the Denver, South Park & Pacific earned the nickname "Damn Slow Pulling and Pretty Rough Riding."

Construction proved difficult. Crews blasted benches into steep mountainsides wide enough to hold the tracks; intricate trestles bridged gullies, some filled with tons of rocks and boulders for safety. Spring meltwater and crumbly rock walls presented constant dangers. From Como to Leadville, the tracks crossed 58 bridges and culverts. Railroad crews worked as quickly as possible. Daniel Curtin in charge of 160 men laid one-half to three-quarters of a mile of track per day on the Blue River extension. Trackmen laid rails of various weights. Between Breckenridge and Dillon, they used 58-pound track (each yard weighed 58 pounds), the heaviest for a narrow- gauge track. In other places, rails 30 feet long and weighing 40 pounds per yard could be used. The men bolted the rails together with fish-plates and spiked them directly to the ties.

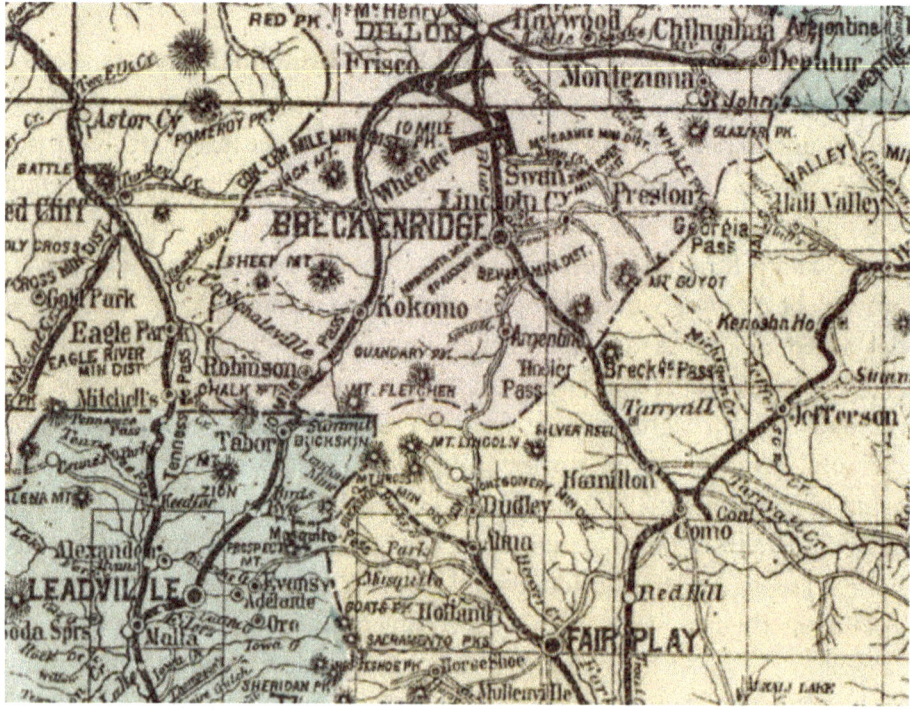

Figure 1-2. Portion of 1882 Map of the Railroad System in Summit, Park, and Lake Counties. Routes extended from Denver to Jefferson, Como, and Fairplay; from Como over Breckenridge Pass to Breckenridge and Frisco; from Dillon to Montezuma; and from Frisco to Kokomo, Robinson, and Leadville. (By Axel Silversparre)

Chapter 1 Overview of Railroads in Summit County

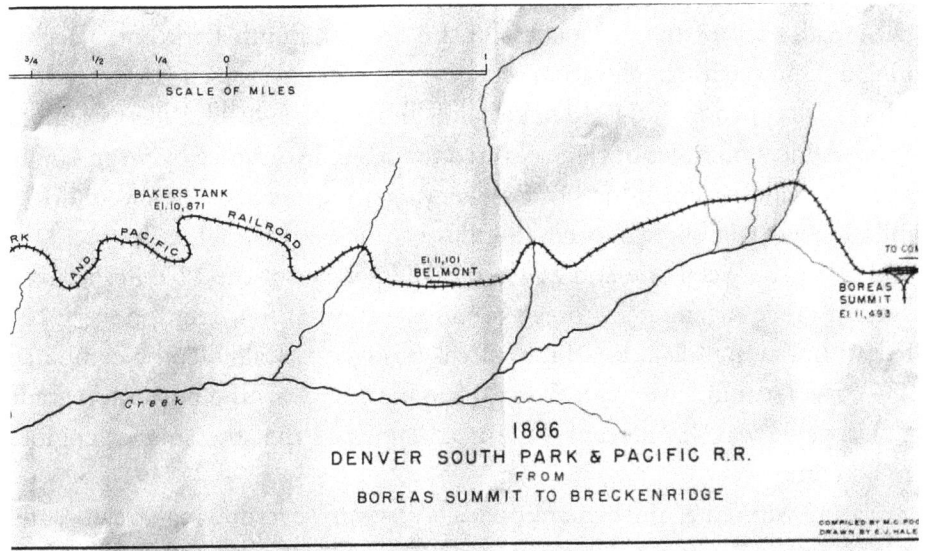

Figure 1-3. DSP&P Highline from Boreas Pass to Bakers Tank, 1886. (Poor, M.C. *Pictorial Supplement to Denver South Park & Pacific*, Denver, Colorado: Rocky Mountain Railroad Club, 1976.)

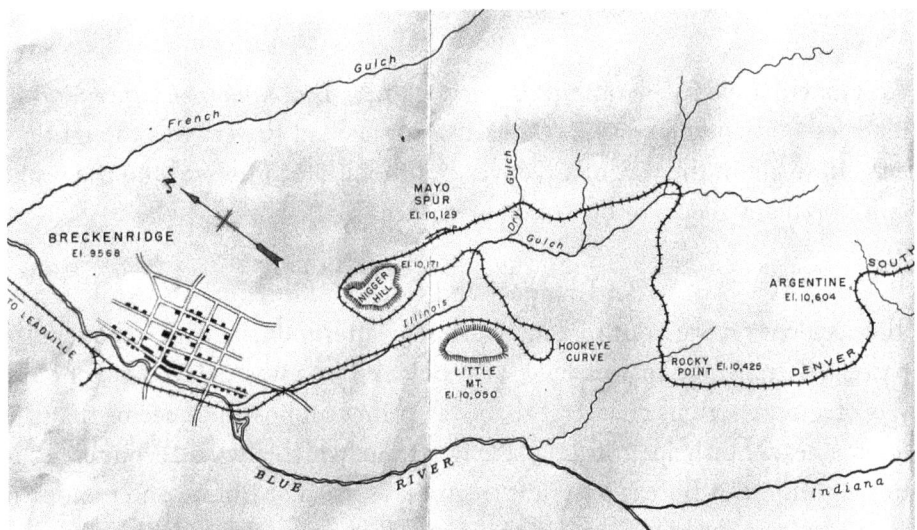

Figure 1-4. DSP&P Highline from Argentine to Breckenridge, 1886. (Poor, M.C. *Pictorial Supplement to Denver South Park & Pacific*, Denver, Colorado: Rocky Mountain Railroad Club, 1976.)

Statistics tell of the uniqueness of the Denver, South Park line. Beginning at Como with an elevation of 9796', the railroad crossed Boreas Pass at 11,481', dropped to 9004' at Dickey and climbed back to 11,108' at Fremont Pass. Almost 63 miles of track covered the 23-mile distance between Como and Leadville. From Boreas to Breckenridge, a distance of six and one-half miles, crews laid slightly over 11 miles of track. Those 11 miles included 108 curves between one and 25 degrees; 82 percent of the 11 miles had a 4 percent grade meaning a drop or rise in elevation of four feet for every 100 feet of horizontal distance. From Breckenridge to Leadville, the combined 234 curves would have made over 16 complete circles. The maximum grade to Leadville was 4.3 percent—the maximum rise that the smaller engines could climb.

Nature worked against the railroads. Washouts, overflowing streams, and rain-softened banks made it extremely difficult to maintain schedules. Bitter cold, howling wind, blowing snow, raging floods, landslides, and avalanches often caused by rumbling engines and shrill whistles increased operating costs and endangered workers, riders, and equipment.

Oops!

Accidents happened—some rather gruesome. The *Summit County Journal* reported on September 15, 1883, that a dog named Rover "was thoughtless enough to get in the way of a Denver, South Park locomotive" and the result "was too many pieces of dog to be of service."

"An Engineer and Fireman Hurt
The accident on the South Park, on Tuesday afternoon, by which the regular passenger train due in Leadville at 6 o'clock p.m., was delayed two hours, was of a more serious character than was at first supposed. It seems that the double header or helper of the passenger train, which always accompanies it to the summit of Boreas pass, left the train as usual at Boreas and ran down ahead of it towards Breckenridge 'light.' When the engine had proceeded about four miles near Farnham station, for some cause, while turning a sharp curve, the engine left the track and turned over, catching the engineer, John Goodhue, underneath. He was quickly rescued from his perilous position;

but not, however, before he and the fireman had sustained serious injuries from the scalding steam, and severe bruises. The injured men were taken back to Como for treatment and the extent of their injuries and bruises is unknown, although believed to be serious." (*The Leadville Daily/Evening Chronicle*, August 25, 1886)

Summit County Winters

The railroads faced the full impact of Summit County winters. Snow, ice, strong winds, and avalanches caused dangerous conditions for crews, equipment, and passengers.

> "The snow and wind has kept the D. L. and G., [Denver, Leadville & Gunnison] people busy keeping the High line open this week. At one time there were eight trains snowed in on Boreas Pass." (*Fairplay Flume*, March 26, 1897)

Keeping the tracks clear of snow, ice, and avalanches could be almost as difficult as laying the tracks in the first place. Of the three, snow presented the biggest problem. Huge wedge-shaped bucking plows, so large they hid the engine behind them, cleared the tracks. With a full head of steam, the engine pushed through the drift until it could go no farther. Then it backed up and tried again until it broke through the drift, hence the term "bucking plow."

For the largest of the drifts, the railroad used a rotary plow, which looked like a fan on the front of a boxcar. The rotating blades threw the snow up to 30 feet away from the tracks. The rotary could blow the snow either to the right or the left, depending on the angle of the rotating blades. Naturally, the company preferred downhill, but if telephone or telegraph poles had been installed on the downhill side of the tracks, snow had to be blown uphill even though it could slide back down on the tracks.

A coal-fired boiler powered the snowplow but the boxcar itself was not self-propelled. As many as six or seven engines pushed the rotary. The last one faced backward to pull the plow out if it should become stuck. Under the rotary plow behind the front wheels, two air-supplied flangers scraped ice off the top and sides of the tracks, preventing the engine from derailing.

Figure 1-5. Plowing Snow between Breckenridge and Keystone. (Courtesy Ed and Nancy Bathke Collection)

Four men operated a rotary snowplow. The pilot sat above and behind the blades, giving him an unobstructed view forward. He communicated with the engineers of the pushing locomotives behind him with whistle signals. Using bells and hand signals, he relayed instructions to his crew, an engineer and two firemen. They decided how fast the rotary should push into the drift and, if necessary, when to reverse direction.

Railroad workers enjoyed telling how a rotary plow had produced instant flying beef steaks as it cut through a huge drift where cattle had frozen to death.

Many snowslides resulted from rumbling engines and shrill train whistles. An avalanche containing trees and rocks rendered the rotary and wedge plows useless. Then dynamite, which could cause another avalanche, and shovelers hired from Denver and Summit County cleared the tracks. If ice and snow remained on the tracks, the next train could derail. Avalanches often created enough damage that rails needed to be repaired or replaced. The shovelers, who cleared the avalanches and repaired the tracks, lived in a boxcar outfitted for eating and sleeping attached behind the last helper engine.

Trains caught behind the rotary or wedge plows continued running to provide heat for the passengers, further draining the railroad's resources.

Figure 1-6. How Deep? The tops of some of the drifts extended far above the top of the rotary snowplow. (Courtesy Ed and Nancy Bathke Collection)

The engineer and fireman did not look forward to riding in the open engine cabs during the winter. They worked with little protection from the weather. The cab on the fireman's side opened to the wind although on some engines, a canvas curtain covered part of the opening. Ice formed on the walls of the cab, while snow covered the deck. Sometimes the ice encrusted the outside of the cab to such a depth that the door could not be opened, trapping the men.

To face the winter weather, with its winds strong enough to blow the coal off the shovel on its way into the fire box and fully loaded cars off the tracks, men wore two sets of woolen underwear, two sets of pants, two shirts, two overalls, two sets of woolen socks, heavy leather boots, a heavy coat, two woolen scarves, a wool cap, and fur-lined gloves.

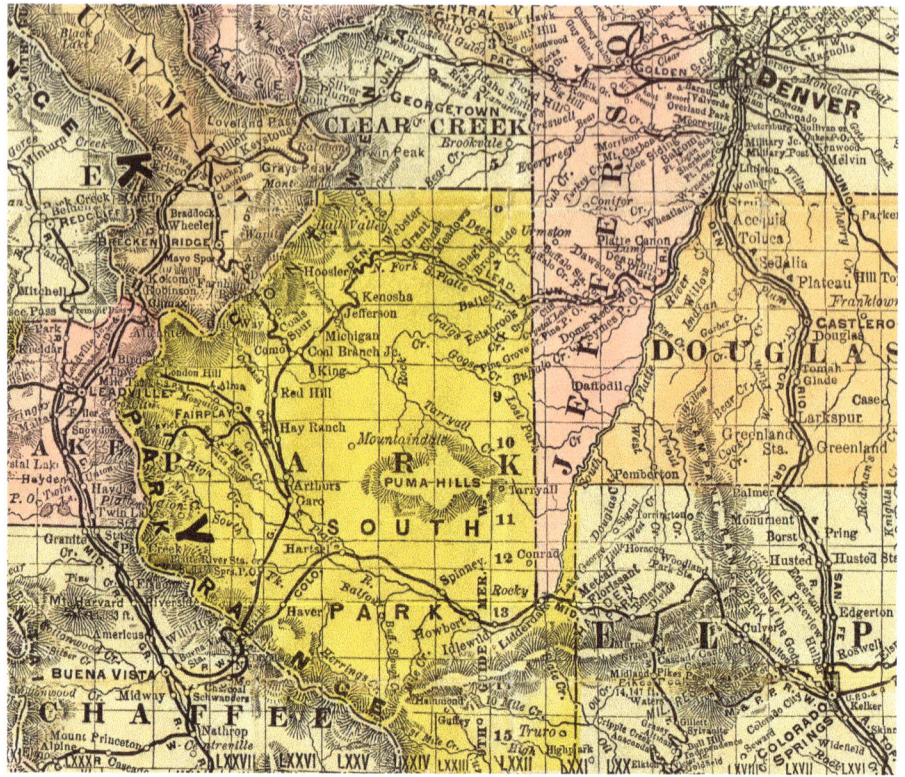

Figure 1-7. Portion of a Railroad Map showing the Routes in Summit and Surrounding Counties, 1898. One route carried passengers and freight from Denver to Leadville, Buena Vista, Colorado Springs, and back to Denver. Another, the High Line, served those in Como, Breckenridge, Dickey, Leadville, and numerous stops in between. (*Rand McNally*)

The Great Blockade

The winter of 1898-1899 surpassed all previous winter snowfall totals. The people of Summit County and the railroad faced particularly difficult conditions. Snow reached impressive depths.

On November 27, 1898, snow began to fall. By the following day, five feet had accumulated. Snow fell almost every day through February 20, 1899. Residents dug tunnels to walk from one side of Main Street to the other.

"The Storm

While during the past two months the mountain section has been visited by an almost continuous storm, that of the past ten days or two weeks has capped the climax, and on Thursday old Boreas bed defiance to every thing human. Since the 14th instant trains on the 'Colorado Road' have been blocked ...

On Tuesday the road officials sent the rotary from Como to Leadville where the regular passenger train was tied up and on Wednesday an attempt was made to get a train from Leadville to Como, but as it had only the flanger along the high winds which had blown since the rotary went through had filled up the track again, the train only succeeded in getting as far as Breckenridge when it was turned back and sent to Leadville to return—well, maybe in the spring." (*Summit County Journal*, January 28, 1899)

Figure 1-8. Leaving Breckenridge, February 5, 1899. Snow prevented the train from reaching Boreas Pass until the following day. (Courtesy Ed and Nancy Bathke Collection)

"A rotary made an attempt to reach Breckenridge this morning but broke down about two miles this side of Boreas pass summit and was compelled to return to Como for repairs." (*Herald Democrat*, Leadville, February 2, 1899)

The last train crossed Boreas Pass on February 6. By February 28, the rotary and wedge plows could no longer keep the tracks clear. Goods entered the county using a sleigh road over the pass. Enough food and other supplies reached Breckenridge to prevent serious shortages, but prices almost doubled at a time when many had no work. Mines furloughed workers because ore could not be shipped. The road proved too soft for heavy ore sleighs.

"On March 2, 75 men with teams of horses braved falling snow to open seven miles of road. More men joined the shovelers on March 3. Merchants Hartman and Foreman provided coffee and food. A week later the men opened a sleigh road to Como. The 18-mile-long road had drifts of snow seven to 15 feet deep. Twelve thousand pounds of mail for Summit County residents had accumulated in Como since the last train made it through." (*Summit County Journal*, March 10, 1899)

In April, the railroad advertised for shovelers to open Boreas Pass. Wages would be $2 per day. Sixty men on April 24 dug from the depot in Breckenridge to the rotary plow stuck on Barney Ford Hill. The blockade lasted 78 days. (*Summit County Journal*, various editions in March and April, 1899)

Dangers

Sparks from the smokestacks of the engines ignited many fires. The *Colorado Daily Chieftain*, Pueblo, noted that "two spans of the Colorado & Southern railway bridge over Illinois gulch, a short distance south of town, were burned yesterday, probably having been fired by a passing engine. All trains were delayed several hours, but passengers and mails were transferred so that traffic was not seriously affected." (June 25, 1902)

Despite deaths and injuries to workers, the Colorado & Southern boasted in 1905 that after 26 years of narrow-gauge rail operations in Summit County, not a single passenger had been killed. (*Summit County Journal*, January 20, 1906) Pure luck played a role in some dangerous situations.

"HAS ANOTHER CLOSE CALL

The lucky star still shines over the South Park division of the C. & S. railroad. On Wednesday afternoon a disastrous and probably fatal accident was narrowly averted on Boreas pass.

On that afternoon, a freight train left Como, west bound, a short while ahead of the passenger train. Coming up the grade, the freight was about two miles ahead of the passenger. At a point about two-thirds of the way up, three empty cars broke loose from the tail-end of the freight train and started back down the steep grade, soon assuming terrible velocity.

Going at hair-raising speed, the 'wild' cars jumped the track on a curve and ran into the bank just in time to ward off an awful collision with the upcoming passenger train.

This is the day of miracles—on the Park road." (*Summit County Journal*, April 21, 1906)

Crew members faced death because of inadequate braking power. Before trains began the descent from Boreas Pass, a brakemen set the brakes so that the trains would not descend at more than five miles per hour. To prevent a "runaway," the brakeman positioned the brakes to drag along the tracks, called "setting the retainers." If needed, the brakes could be lowered to provide more drag. A train descending a 4.5 percent grade doubled its speed every 15 seconds unless checked by strong brakes.

In November, 1907, two loaded freight cars with loosened automatic brake rods rolled from Kokomo to Frisco in 42 minutes, eventually colliding and spilling clothing along the right-of-way. (*Summit County Journal*, November 23, 1907)

"C.& S. TRAIN DASHES DOWN STEEP GRADE
Sixteen Cars Destroyed on South Park Division; Engineer Decapitated; Crew Saved by Jumping.

COMO, Colo., March 20—After running uncontrolled down the steep grade from Boreas pass on the crest of the Continental divide a Colorado & Southern freight train composed of sixteen cars loaded with ore left the rails four miles from here last night and went into the ditch. Oswald B. Schwartz, the engineer, was instantly killed. All other members of the train crew jumped when they saw that to stop the train was impossible.

The accident occurred on the South Park branch of the Colorado & Southern and trains are lowered down the slope with the utmost difficulty, owing to the steep grade. In stormy weather when the rails are most frequent runaways have occurred.

Schwartz was one of the oldest engineers in the service of the Colorado & Southern. He had been in eight wrecks and had escaped unscratched. Last night when the heavily loaded train began slipping on him and gradually increased its momentum he remained at his post of duty and repeatedly did everything in his power to decrease the rapid flight. The train had run five miles and had attained a speed of ninety miles an hour when in rounding a sharp curve the engine and tender and sixteen cars left the rails. So fast was the train going that the cars were piled in one huge heap forty feet from the roadbed. The track was not damaged and traffic continued without delay.

The body of Schwarz was found in the ruins of his engine. He had been literally decapitated, only two cords of his neck connecting the head and body. None of the other members of the crew were injured, as they had jumped into the soft snow." (*The Aspen Daily Times*, March 21, 1909)

"WHY ENGINEER GAVE UP LIFE

An investigation conducted by the Colorado & Southern yesterday to determine the cause of the wreck of a runaway train Friday night on Boreas pass has brought to light acts of heroism which will add new laurels to the record of Colorado railroad men.

Bud Schwartz, the engineer who went to his death because he believed it was his duty refused to listen to the pleadings of the fireman to jump and save his life and the fireman came very near meeting death as a result of his efforts to save the engineer.

The investigation was conducted in the office of Superintendent Bacon at the Union Depot and was the regulation hearing made upon all accidents. B. A. Ingledew, the fireman on the ill-fated train, whose family resides in Denver, was one of the principal witnesses. The train which was loaded with sixteen cars of ore, became unmanageable about 11 o'clock Friday night while descending Boreas pass on the crest of the continental divide. When it was seen that nothing could stop the train . . . the crew all jumped except Engineer Schwartz, who declined to leave his post and went to his death."

Before railroad companies installed more-reliable Westinghouse brakes on rolling stock, brakemen had to depend on Eames vacuum brakes that often failed on the steep slopes, resulting in runaway trains. If the train crew felt it could no longer control the train and it was unsafe to stay on-board, they made the dangerous decision to jump. The reporter continued the story:

"The investigation shows that Ingledew realized the danger and made an effort to get Schwartz to jump. Schwartz refused. The momentum of the train was increasing every minute and it was making about seventy-five miles an hour at the time. Ingledew left his seat and went to the engineer's side, taking him by the arm and pleading with him to jump as it was his only hope. While begging his companion to save his life Ingledew was himself momentarily approaching death. At last he made a final effort and the engineer shook his head. He had determined to die at his post in an effort to stop the train. Ingledew bade him good-by and went to the side of the cab to leap. On one side was the precipitous cliffs, which would have meant instant death and it looked as if he had waited too long for his own safety. He then went to the engineer's side of the cab and leaped into the dark. He landed in a bed of snow and escaped with only a few bruises. The train had gone only a few feet after he leaped before it jumped the track and carried the engineer to his death. Twenty seconds more and the fireman would have died by his side." (*The Daily Sentinal*, Grand Junction, March 26, 1909)

Some tragedies had happy endings. "As a coal train descended Barney Ford Hill, the engineer and fireman, thinking the train was a 'runaway,' jumped after reversing the engine. The conductor and brakeman set the brakes on the caboose, then climbed over the cars setting the brakes on each by hand. The train finally stopped at the Adams Avenue crossing. Fifteen minutes later, the engineer and brakeman came running along the tracks surprised to see their train in one piece." (*Summit County Journal*, April 10, 1909)

A very dangerous situation occurred on March 2, 1909, when ice from water leaking from Bakers Tank covered the tracks near Boreas Pass. While water in the tanks usually did not freeze, leaks along the seams caused some magnificent ice fountains beside and sometimes on the tracks. When the water tank in Dickey froze in 1912, firemen used a hose attached to a fire plug on Main Street in Breckenridge to "water" the engines. To prevent water in the tender from freezing, the firemen diverted some of the hot water from the engine boiler into the 2,500-gallon tender.

Déjà vu

When snow prevented a train from reaching its destination, passengers faced the decision of remaining with the train or trudging through deep snow.

"Still We Are Snow Bound
On last Saturday the C. & S. put several engines and a gang of thirty shovelers to work opening up the High Line, and travel was resumed late that evening. Another storm immediately came on,

and we have been isolated from the world since Monday. Tuesday's east bound train, with four engines, was stalled on Boreas pass and it took more than two days to force its way through to Como, assisted by a crew of shovelers ... Most of its passengers deserted it on Wednesday and walked ten miles to Como ... several ladies, including Miss Lillie Bruch, of Breckenridge, stayed in the cars till the end." (*Summit County Journal*, February 27, 1909)

Another reporter told it differently.

"Snowbound on Boreas Pass
Denver—A Republican special from Breckenridge Wednesday night says: The eastbound Colorado & Southern passenger train No. 72 left here yesterday at noon with four locomotives for Como and Denver. After leaving Boreas station the train was stalled by the drifted snow. After spending the night on top of the range the male passengers decided to walk the eight or nine miles separating them from Como, where they arrived safely this afternoon.

The only lady passenger, Miss Lillian Bruch, a nurse from St. Luke's hospital of Denver, who was returning from a visit to her parents here, decided to trust herself to the tender mercies of the Boreas section house rather than wade through miles of drifted snow." (*Turret Gold Belt*, Turret, Chaffee County, March 3, 1909)

The Blockade of 1923

The winter of 1923 brought back memories of the winter of 1899. Seven slides of ice, rocks, and trees from 500 to several thousand feet long and 15 to 50 feet deep south of Curtin in the Ten Mile Canyon blocked the Colorado & Southern line to Leadville. Drifts towered over the rotary. Shovelers worked on the tops of the drifts, lowering them to the size that the snowplow could remove by shoveling the snow onto the tracks where the rotary could throw the snow up and over the top of the downhill side of the drift.

Figure 1-9. Train blocked by an Avalanche near Curtin in Ten Mile Canyon, March, 1923. (Robert H. Sayre Collection [cou-bha BHA.0007]; Courtesy Breckenridge History)

Figure 1-10. Avalanche totally blocking the Track, Curtin, 1923. (Robert H. Sayre Collection [cou-bha BHA.0007]; Courtesy Breckenridge History)

Chapter 1 Overview of Railroads in Summit County

Figure 1-11. Avalanche cleared by Rotary in Ten Mile Canyon. (Courtesy Maureen Nicholls)

The railroad made little effort to keep the Boreas Pass route open. Residents endured shortages of butter, eggs, flour, sugar, meat, and other necessities. By this time, the railroad had little incentive to keep the tracks clear. Profits had been shrinking for years. Cars and trucks carried more of the ore and other goods the railroads had carried. The railroad had abandoned Boreas Pass in 1910 and only reopened it because of a 1913 court order.

Trains finally arrived ending the 11-day blockage from the east and two-week blockade from the west. The first trains needed four hours to travel from Rocky Point to the Breckenridge depot, a usual trip of about 25 minutes covering about five and one-half miles.

Financial Problems from the Beginning

From its inception, the High Line faced financial difficulties because of inadequate funding. At the turn of the century, those financial problems dictated corporate changes. Reorganizing to avoid bankruptcy, the Denver, South Park & Pacific (commonly referred to as just the Denver, South Park) became the Denver, Leadville & Gunnison Railway Company in 1889. First the Colorado & Southern (C&S) in 1898 and then the Chicago, Burlington & Quincy in 1908 purchased the struggling company. These owners had little interest in maintaining the narrow-gauge line because of high operating expenses. The county's mines produced little high-grade ore. As was true throughout the entire mining era of Summit County, low-grade ore prevailed. The newest concentration methods resulted in even less to carry. In addition, electricity, available in Breckenridge in 1898 and in Frisco and Dillon in 1909, reduced the need for coal, which had always been a big part of the tonnage carried on incoming trains. The inability to integrate narrow- and standard-gauge rolling stock created further difficulties for the company. To compound the problem, cars, trucks, and buses began replacing the railroad as the primary carrier of people and freight.

As early as 1900, rumors of abandonment had been swirling:

> "During the past few months all sorts of rumors have been floating around—and some of them received publicity in the press—to the effect that the consolidation of the Midland and Colorado & Southern would as a matter of course, result in the abandonment of the high line, between Como and Breckenridge, during the snowy winter months.
>
> To arrive at the real facts in the matter, a representative of the JOURNAL on Tuesday interviewed General Superintendent Dyer on the subject. In reply, the clever official assured us that the project of allowing the Boreas Pass line to snow up was never seriously considered by the C. & S.; that estimates were now being considered for and a string of new snow sheds would be constructed on Boreas pass ere the snowy season sets in, and that additional precautionary measures were to be taken to keep the road open. Finally, he added that it was the policy of the C. & S. to buy, build and extend lines instead of abandoning any it already owned." (*Summit County Journal*, August 11, 1900)

The railroad followed through with its plans to fight the storms of winter:

"PREPARE FOR WINTER—The Colorado & Southern railway is making extensive improvements on its road in contemplation of any heavy snows that may come this winter and to prevent any such serious interference with traffic as occurred in the winter of 1898-1899. Several cars of material were sent out yesterday and the company has purchased several hundred thousand feet of lumber for the purpose of building new snow sheds on the Boreas Pass route. Work has already begun and will be completed before the cold weather sets in." (*Herald Democrat*, September 26, 1900)

The railroad continued upgrading the line:

"On the Fix-up
The visionary theories of the know-alls relative to the abandonment of a portion of the South Park one by the C. & S. people are now effectually squelched. At present the Colorado & Southern has a large force of laborers on the High Line placing the track in better condition and 'fixing things up' generally, and the improvements are made with a view to permanency.

Among the new things now receiving attention we notice . . . a 12-pocket elevated coal-chute at Dickey, which will enable engines to coal in one minute; the station buildings along the line, especially those at Dillon and Breckenridge, have undergone thorough repairs and the painting gang is now recoating them with a bright red . . ." (*Summit County Journal*, July 27, 1901)

The railroad faced repeated fires caused by sparks from engines passing through the snowsheds. They proposed a novel experiment but never followed through with their idea, despite the report:

"Railroad Grade Changed
The Colorado & Southern railway company will try an experi-

ment on the Atlantic slope of Boreas pass this winter. For years the expense of snowshedding that side of the pass has been an enormous annual drain on the treasury. Nearly every summer one or more snowsheds burned down and had to be rebuilt. As snowsheds burned down and had to be rebuilt. As snowsheds cost about $7 a running foot the company has hit upon a new plan, and instead of rebuilding the 1,800 foot shed which went up in smoke a few months ago, the location of the track was changed and the track raised, on the assumption that the snow would blow off of the new roadbed." (*Summit County Journal*, October 14, 1905)

But just a few years later, responding to declining profits, the railroads announced their intention to vacate the county.

> "LEADVILLE BRANCH TO BE DISCONTINUED
> The South Park branch of the Colorado and Southern railway, running between Denver and Leadville, is to be abandoned according to reports from Breckenridge, the largest town on that division east of Leadville. October 1, when the tourist business is at an end and when the winter practically begins in that section is given as the date for the cessation of traffic over the line.
>
> Officials of the Colorado & Southern admit that this division has never paid [made a profit] although it was the first railroad into Leadville and in its early day did a large business. For the past ten years it has cost, according to these officials, $200,000 a year more than its gross earnings, and this fact has led to the determination to abandon it, as it is the policy of James J. Hill who controls the Colorado and Southern, to drop lines which fail to show a credit on the ledgers every year, or which fail to develop territory traversed. In both respects the old South Park division has come short . . .West of Como as far as Breckenridge there is nothing except tanks and spurs which ran to what were formerly lumber camps and occasionally a mine, but which are now worked out. Between Breckenridge and Leadville are several towns, including

Dillon, and Kokomo, and these, it is said could be served better if the line to Denver were abandoned and the section from Leadville to Breckenridge with more assurance of continuity of service by way of Leadville . . .

Aside from the lack of freight and passenger traffic between Denver and Leadville, maintenance of train service is extremely expensive on account of the heavy grades and the constant danger of snow blockades for six months of the year . . .

When the Denver, South Park & Pacific was chartered the company stipulated that it would maintain train service at all times and that no part of the line would be abandoned, and this provision of law may operate to save the line. However, other railroads which had similar requirements in their charters have found a way to drop unremunerative lines, and it is probable that the legal department of the Colorado & Southern will discover some means of encompassing the abandonment of this one." (*Montrose Daily Press*, August 25, 1910)

In spite of what appeared to be a profitable year for the railroads, Denver, Rio Grande stopped service on its Ten Mile Canyon line in February, 1911, saying it could no longer afford to duplicate the services offered by Colorado & Southern. This left only one railroad serving Summit County and it wanted to drop its line over Boreas Pass routing all freight and passengers through Leadville. The newspaper editor complained that C&S had "Breckenridge to a whipping post; lives were imperiled and business suffered." He called the railroad "flat wheeled, stub toe and stick in the snow."

Service resumed but people had reservations:

> "SERVICE VIA COMO TO RESUME APRIL 1
> ". . . What kind of a train the Colorado & Southern intend to put on, whether it will be an intermittent freight train with a couple of dingy, dinky, poorly-lighted, patched-up 'Jim Crow' passenger boxes dragging along in the rear . . .

Will our train service over Boreas Pass be resumed with the same satisfaction we formerly experienced, or does the promise mean that once a week or twice a week or at their convenience the C.& S. will run their train?" (*The Summit County Journal & Breckenridge Bulletin*, March 18, 1911)

To fight the railroad's efforts to abandon the line, residents of Breckenridge formed the Breckenridge Chamber of Commerce.

". . . The Colorado & Southern railroad is about to resume its service over Boreas pass on the South Park line, and we believe the doubters and grumblers will be surprised when the through service from Leadville is soon established. But the point is for us now to get together, to have a Chamber of Commerce, a Board of Trade or a Commercial Club, where we can invite agricultural and mining men to speak now and then, where we can discuss in unison the wants we are aware of, and where we can throw our whole commercial and individual power into our demands for the righting of a wrong or the prevention of an injustice . . ." (*The Summit County Journal & Breckenridge Bulletin*, April 1, 1911)

"CHAMBER OF COMMERCE A BIG REALITY
Representative and Enthusiastic Citizens' Meeting Has Called It Into Being
STARTS OFF AUSPICIOUS

The Breckenridge Chamber of Commerce is organized! Breckenridge has awakened! The individual moral and physical support of every Breckenridge business man and citizen which this paper pleaded for when the commercial body was proposed burst forth spontaneously last Monday night in the county court room of our stately county building, where the most enthusiastic mass meeting Summit county has seen for years was participated in by men who realized the necessity of launching an organization of this kind at once and doing it successfully . . .

. . . It took about fifteen minutes to elect the following officers: President, Fred C. Cramer, treasurer for the town of Breckenridge and county surveyor; first vice president, Theodore H. Knorr, a well known mining and business man; second vice president, Hon. C. L. Westerman, a retired business man and a recognized 'booster'; treasurer, W. F. Forman, who has been county clerk and recorder for over thirty years; secretary, S. S. Fry, a professional man of Breckenridge.

The board of directors, chosen unanimously, as were the other officers, consist of W. H. Briggle, assistant cashier of Engle Bros.' Exchange Bank, ex-mayor of Breckenridge, and a gentleman we are proud to know; R. M. Henderson, manager of the Wellington Mines company, under whose practical management this great company has become a dividend payer; George Robinson, county treasurer, whose efficient direction of the county's financial affairs has gained for him the confidence of every one who knows him; George C. Smith, a business man of Breckenridge, whose extensive mining experience and knowledge of mining conditions in Summit county will be most useful to the Chamber of Commerce in regulating listed claims; Dr. E. W. Shrock, dentist and property-holder, who is a 'booster' of the first water and whose enthusiasm helped make the Breckenridge Chamber of Commerce an actuality." (*The Summit County Journal & Breckenridge Bulletin*, April 22, 1911)

The group decided on a membership fee of $1 per month and met in the *Journal* office.

Despite the efforts of the new Chamber and other organizations in both Summit County and Denver, the railroad continued its efforts to completely or partially curtail service.

"LINE ABANDONED ON BOREAS PASS
People of Breckenridge Again Up in Arms and
Also Complain About Mail Facilities

. . . The C. & S. people abandoned the road [rail line] from Como to this place on Wednesday evening by telegraphic orders giving no previous notification whatever. It may be that the railroad people know what they are doing and how this will terminate and again they may not . . .

The railroad people claim the deep snow on Boreas was the cause of their shutting down the road. As a matter of fact there is less snow than there has been for years, no snow to bother at all." (*Herald Democrat*, Leadville, January 9, 1912)

Cases heard by the Colorado Railroad Commission, District Court, and Colorado Supreme Court prevented the total stoppage of service. When justices refused to rule in its favor, the railroad would open the line but often increased freight rates and passenger fares.

"Over Boreas Pass
AFTER an abandonment of little over a year, during which time a fierce legal battle fought over the matter through several courts the Colorado & Southern Railway company re-established through train service over the South Park branch between Denver and Leadville on Monday, January 20, 1913, on the terms of the order of the state railroad commission issued on November 29, 1911, and calling for the operation and maintenance of 'a through and exclusive passenger train service daily, excepting Sunday, from Denver to Leadville by the way of Como and Breckenridge,' and a similar passenger service in the opposite direction; also for the maintenance and operations of 'a through freight service from Denver to Leadville' over the same route, at least three days each week, in both directions." (*Blue Valley Times*, Dillon, January 24, 1913)

Intermittent stoppages of service continued. Lawyers filed appeals: U.S. Supreme Court, Colorado Public Utilities Commission, Interstate Commerce Commission in 1921, and the Interstate Commerce Commission in 1928. The county won. The ICC ruled that the miners and ranchers deserved railroad service but added that unless the people in the county increased the business given to the railroad in the next three years, the railroad would be allowed to file another petition for abandonment. As expected, a few months later, the railroad filed a petition with the state PUC asking to curtail service. Denying the petition, the PUC ruled that it would not grant the request for abandonment until the railroad made an effort to modernize its equipment. The railroad, the PUC felt, created its own problems by using "ancient" locomotives and rolling stock thereby increasing operating expenses and decreasing business.

As many would have predicted, C&S finally received permission to abandon the Boreas Pass line based on the fact that trucks now carried half of the county's freight.

The railroad had planned to stop service Friday, December 11, 1936, but the ICC ruling included the stipulation that the railroad must continue operating for four more months until April 12, 1937. If by that time business had increased significantly, the ICC would not allow abandonment. Instead of making improvements to increase business, the railroad continued using inefficient, expensive, and old equipment, driving up costs and driving away business.

After trying since 1911, the Colorado & Southern finally abandoned its lines in 1937. *The Denver Post* on Friday, April 9, 1937, reported:

> "The Last Train leaves Denver on Famous Leadville Line.
> Return on Saturday will end traffic on road closely lined with romantic period in history of Colorado.
> One coach, one baggage car, and a tiny locomotive stood in the frosty shadows of two big modern trains at the Union Station, early Friday morning loading a few passengers and some small freight, mostly groceries for the last trip out of Denver on one of the most romantic railroads in the west."

Crews removed rails and ties the following year. Only the 14 miles of narrow-gauge track running from Climax to Leadville remained to carry the mineral molybdenum. The Colorado & Southern converted them to standard gauge on August 25, 1943.

Authors' Note: For a detailed review of the railroad's efforts to abandon service in Summit County, see *Roadside Summit, Part II* by Pritchard Mather.

Benefits

Figure 1-12. Dismantling the High Line, 1938. The train with two engines and two flatbed cars hauled away the salvaged track. (Denver Public Library, Western History Collection, DPL OP-6229)

Figure 1-13. Removing Track between Breckenridge and Boreas Pass. (Courtesy Denver, South Park & Pacific Historical Society Collection)

Chapter 1 Overview of Railroads in Summit County

Figure 1-14. C&S Employees removing Rails, Spikes, Tie Plates, and Rail Fish Plates. The men slid the salvaged rails up the ramp to a flatbed car pulled by engines No. 69 and No. 58. (Courtesy Jackson Thode Photo, Tom Klinger Collection)

It is impossible to overestimate the importance of the railroads to Summit County's people and economy. They tied sawmills, mines, and ranches to distant markets. Ore trains needed only one day to reach smelters in Denver. Lower grade ores could be shipped at a profit.

The railroad carried potatoes, cattle to Omaha and Denver, sheep, mail, coal for the train itself as well as for homes and dredges, fish to stock lakes and streams, hardware, luxuries such as phonographs and records, charcoal produced in the county for Denver markets, ore, railroad ties, logs and lumber, food, clothing, mining equipment too large for wagons, and even a carload of empty whiskey bottles sent from the Denver House in Breckenridge to Denver to be refilled.

The railroad allowed the people of Summit County to take advantage of the services in Denver and Leadville. It provided an opportunity for those in the county to see the "outside world" and encouraged visitors to enjoy the natural beauty of Summit County.

"RAILROAD PEOPLE SHOW A FRIENDLY DISPOSITION

Colorado & Southern After Several Years of Bitter Fighting Decides to Advertise Breckenridge, and More is Much Appreciated Locally.

The Colorado and Southern Railway is advertising Breckenridge in the Denver papers with an ad which reads as follows: 'To Breckenridge or Leadville over the Scenic South Park Line.—A famous trip through picturesque Platte Canon to a nationally celebrated mining section through a wilderness of canons and peaks. A trip every Colorado visitor should make. Via Colorado & Southern railway.'

There are two excellent points brought out in the advertisement. The trip is one that every Colorado visitor should make. It is probably the most picturesque trip of equal distance in Colorado. It is far prettier than some of the much advertised trips that are looked forward to by prospective Colorado visitors. There is a greater

variety of scenery than any other trip of equal distance affords
... Then the climb of the continental divide, through the snow
at Boreas Pass, and down the beautiful valley of the Blue. Past
productive mines that are turning out precious metals, immense
dredge boats gathering the gold nuggets from the river bed,
around Breckenridge, down the Blue to Dillon in a fine farming
community, then the Ten Mile river with more picturesque
scenery passing through Kokomo a prosperous camp of the early
days over the pass at Climax . . . It is the one trip that should
be taken by all tourists who visit Colorado.' " (*Summit County Journal*, July 17, 1915)

The railroads played a major role in determining the location of a town and its businesses. Once the railroad arrived, businesses moved to trackside and geared business operations, sometimes involuntarily, to the delivery schedule of the railroads. In 1921, the *Summit County Journal* complained that "because of a delay in the delivery of paper from the Western Newspaper Union routed by way of Utah, Mexico or China, or some other nearby points by the Colorado and Southern," the *Journal* would be late. Unloading facilities, coal bins, smelters, and mills lined the tracks. Coal, comprising a large part of the tonnage carried by the railroads, came from the King and Baldwin mines near Gunnison. Owned by the Union Pacific Railroad, they provided coal for mines, smelters, and train locomotives.

The railroad created the "other side of the tracks." Cribs inhabited by "ladies of the night" lined the tracks—even in Breckenridge where maps showed dwellings in which "boarders" lived.

The railroad changed the simple diets of the miners and their families. Previously, professional hunters, receiving ten cents per pound for elk and buffalo, supplied much of the meat eaten by the miners. The railroad brought fresh meat in Tiffany refrigerator cars kept cold by blocks of ice. Vegetables and fruit, some coming from the Mormon settlements in Utah, augmented diets. Markets offered oysters, apple juice, fresh carrots, cranberries, and red beets.

Railroads, because of their need to maintain schedules, introduced standard time to towns along the tracks. Before 1882, Breckenridge used the sun or clocks at the Gold Pan Shops for telling time.

Even so, the railroad was not the panacea many expected. While railroads did lower the cost of living, allow mines with ores of lesser value to continue operating, end the isolation of the county, and haul ores and agricultural products to market rapidly, the rates remained excessively high in the eyes of many.

The demise of the railroad can be attributed to a variety of items: the failure of the railroad to develop new business; the lack of investment in more efficient engines and rolling stock; the decline of the mining industry; the lack of financial backing by investors; the use of electricity in mines reducing the need for coal; the inability to integrate the narrow-gauge equipment with standard-gauge lines; and the growth of the highway system with trucks, personal cars, and buses.

Gone are the thundering steam engines rumbling along their tracks and rotary snowplows attacking huge avalanches and snow drifts. But the need for cheap, efficient transportation, once so critical to the mining and ranching economies, still remains central to Summit County's economy, now based on summer and winter recreation.

CHAPTER 2
BOREAS PASS STATION

Site Location

Boreas Pass—milepost 98.84, elevation 11,481 feet—named for the Greek God of the North Wind by Sidney Dillon—yes, that Sydney Dillon, president of the Union Pacific and person for whom the town of Dillon, Colorado, was named. Boreas Pass—formerly Breckenridge Pass, honoring Thomas E. Breckenridge, who lost his mule at the pass, and person for whom the town of Breckenridge was named.

Built in 1882 by the railroad for their employees and families, who endured raging winds and howling snow every month of the year, it held the distinction of being the highest rail station in the United States.

Figure 2-1. Boreas Pass, circa 1900. The large two-story building on the right served as the station house. (Courtesy Maureen Nicholls)

Figure 2-2. Portion of 1898 Map with Boreas Station. (*Rand McNally*)

Boreas Pass straddles the continental divide. Crofutt in 1885 explained it this way: "Here the waters divide. Should a bucket full of Adam's ale be emptied on the summit of this grand ridge it would separate, one portion finding its way to the Gulf of Mexico and the other to the Gulf of California." (*Crofutt's Grip Sack Guide of Colorado*, 1885)

Designated Station No. 1133, at milepost 98.84, the settlement lined the DSP&P tracks. A depot, storehouse with dirt roof, telegraph house, and section house stood on the east side of the tracks. The storehouse and section house still stand.

In 1883, workers built a stone engine house with turntable, coal bin, and water tank fed by springs on the west side of the road. Destroyed by fire in 1909, only the foundation of the engine house remains. Pieces of coal indicate the location of the coal bin; portions of the turntable foundation have survived.

Figure 2-3. Boreas Pass Stone Engine House, circa 1880s. (Courtesy Maureen Nicholls)

Figure 2-4. Boreas Pass Stone Engine House, circa 1900. (Photograph by Clinton H Scott, Courtesy Maureen Nicholls)

Figure 2-5. Engine House after Fire, 1909. The fire gutted the engine house and burned the roof. The intense heat twisted the tracks inside. Over the succeeding years, the rock walls collapsed into a pile of rubble. (Courtesy Maureen Nicholls)

Figure 2-6. Boreas Pass Stone Engine House, 1920s. Locals removed some of the stones in the walls, using them for a variety of purposes. (Jim Woodward Collection, Courtesy Gloria Swan Berkely)

Rock Quarry

An 1882 USGS map and F.C. Cramer's 1908 map show a rock quarry located southwest of Boreas Pass (**Figures 2-7, 2-8**). When Fountain investigated, he surmised that railroad construction crews used stone from the quarry to build the Boreas Pass engine house. On June 28, 2022, Fountain and Robin Theobald explored the quarry and located five areas where crews had removed rocks. (**Figures 2-9 through 9-16**)

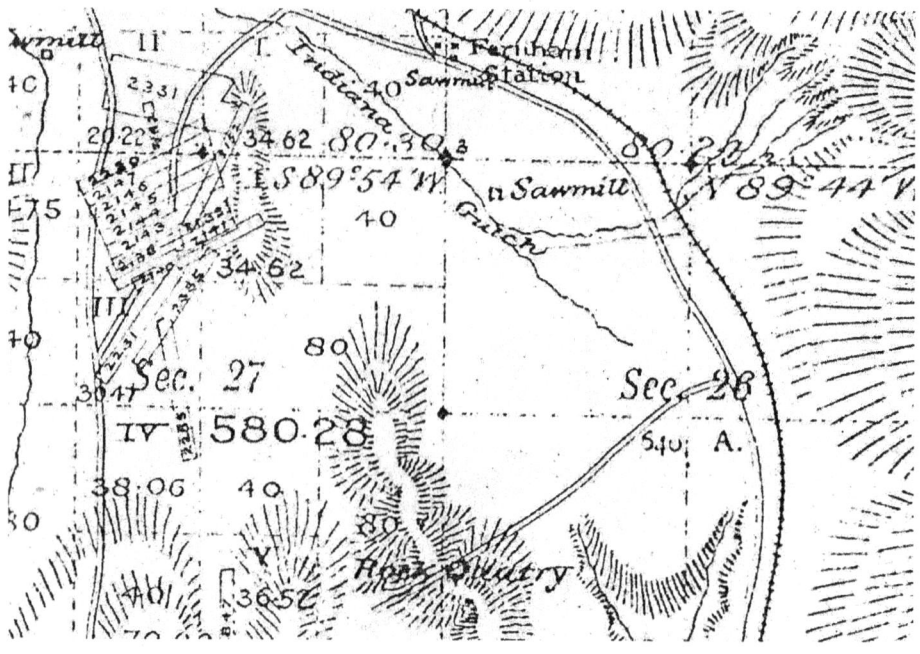

Figure 2-7. Portion of an 1882 USGS Map indicating the Road leading to the Rock Quarry near Boreas Pass. Originally known as Breckenridge Pass, the pass became Boreas Pass a short time later when Sidney Dillon, the president of the Union Pacific, changed it to honor the Greek God of the North Wind.

Figure 2-8. Portion of a 1908 F.C. Cramer Map with the Pass and Road leading to the Rock Quarry. (Topographical Map of the Blue River Gold Field and Metal Mines, Summit County, Colorado)

Figure 2-9. Looking up the Hill from Boreas Pass to the Rock Quarries. Note the raised area on the ridge on the right. (Photograph by Author)

Figure 2-10. Rock Quarry No. 1 on the South Side of the Ridge. Fountain numbered the quarries; No. 1 being the largest. The rocks came from the rust-colored area to the right. (Photograph by Author)

Figure 2-11. Close-Up View of Rock Quarry No. 1. (Photograph by Author)

Figure 2-12. Snow in Rock Quarry No. 1, June 28, 2022. The quarried rock face appears on the left. For an unknown reason, workers constructed a rock wall to form a pit. Note the Boreas Pass station house in the distance. (Photograph by Author)

Figure 2-13. Approaching Rock Quarry No. 2 and Discarded Boulders. This quarry was located south of and at a slightly lower elevation than Rock Quarry No. 1. (Photograph by Author)

Figure 2-14. Rock Face, Quarry No. 2. Note the 12 shallow drill holes at the top of the sharp rock face. (Photograph by Author)

Figure 2-15. Rock Quarry No. 3 on North Side of Hill. (Photograph by Author)

Chapter 2 Boreas Pass Station

Figure 2-16. Rock Quarry No. 4. Crews took rock from the depression between the two reddish rock faces. (Photograph by Author)

Remains of Engine House

Figure 2-17. All that Remained of the Stone Engine House, 1975. (Courtesy of the Summit Historical Society)

Figure 2-18. Remnants of the Stone Engine House, 2022. (Photograph by Author)

Roundhouse in Como

In 1881, Denver, South Park & Pacific built the roundhouse in Como with rock that most likely came from the rock quarry on Boreas Pass.

Figure 2-19. Como Roundhouse with Four Locomotives Inside and One Outside. The turntable directed the engines into individual stalls. The rocks most likely came from the rock quarry on Boreas Pass, 1886. (Denver, South Park & Pacific Historical Society Collection)

Figure 2-20. Rear, Exterior of the Como Roundhouse, March, 1951. (Denver, South Park & Pacific Historical Society Collection)

Figure 2-21. The Como Roundhouse, 1970s. (Courtesy Maureen Nicholls)

Snowsheds

To counter the winds and deep snow, the railroad constructed snowsheds over the tracks. The first, built in 1885, measured 600 feet. In 1898, the year of the Big Blockade, workers attached the depot to the snowshed so riders could exit the train in the snowshed and walk directly into the depot. When the snowshed burned a year later, in 1899, the railroad rebuilt it and lengthened it to 997 feet. Logs from the wooden depot foundation still lay buried in the ground next to the road. Another snowshed partially covered 1566 feet of sidetrack and the wye used to turn helper engines.

The grade for the wye extends west of the engine house foundation; willows hide some ties from a spur east of the road. Wagon ruts lead north from the section house.

Figure 2-22. Snowshed on Boreas Pass, 1885. The stone engine house appears to the right of the snowshed. The large, two-story section house stood to the left. (Courtesy Maureen Nicholls)

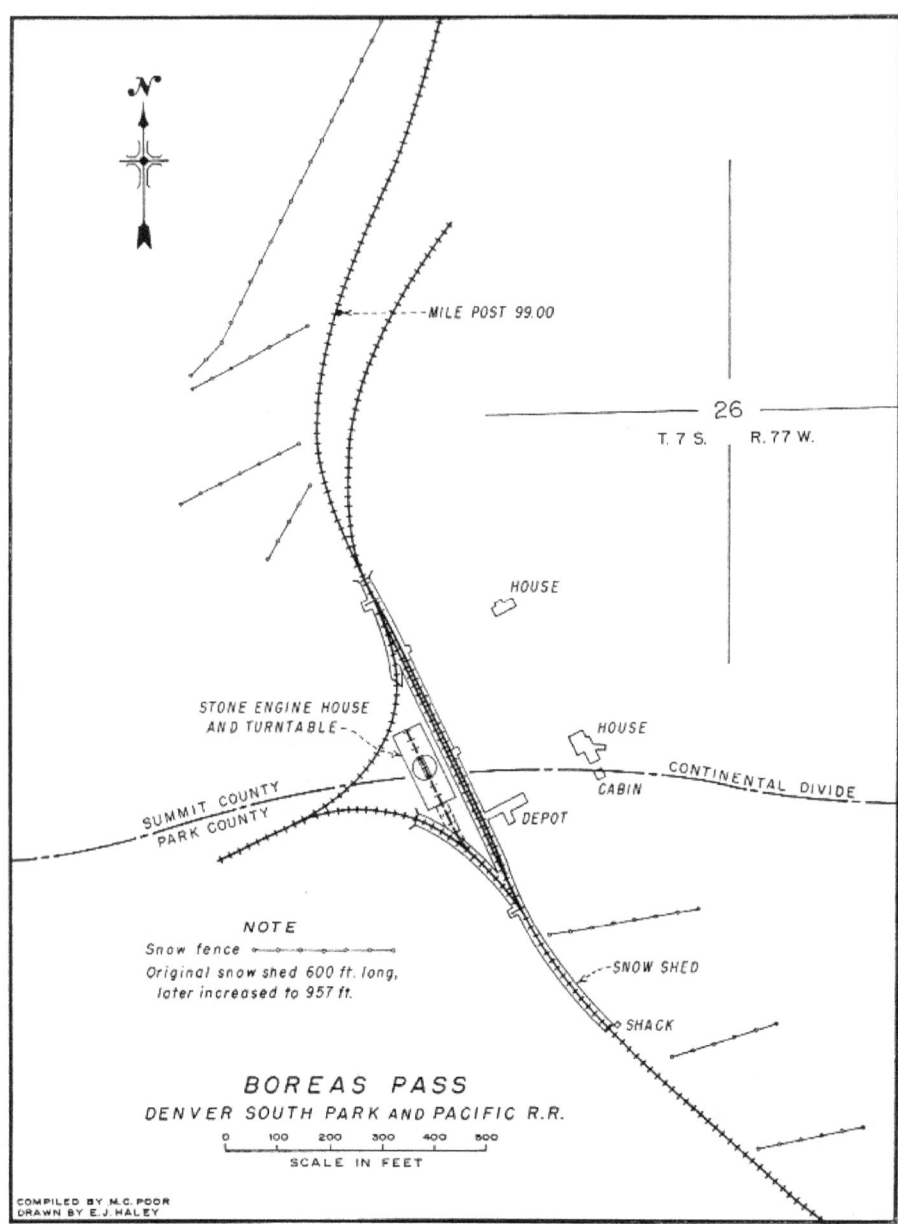

Figure 2-23. Map of Railroad Buildings and Trackage at Boreas Pass. The wye, which allowed helper engines to reverse direction, straddled the stone engine house. Long snow fences west of the main line kept drifting snow from burying the tracks and spur. (From *Denver South Park & Pacific*, M.C. Poor)

Chapter 2 Boreas Pass Station

Figure 2-24. Boreas Station House and Storehouse, 1890s. (Denver, South Park & Pacific Historical Society Collection)

Although no businesses operated at Boreas station, the settlement received a post office on January 2, 1896, with John W. Soper serving as postmaster. The train carried literally "tons" for mail to Breckenridge residents and a steady stream of passengers who conducted business in Breckenridge and patronized the merchants. But travelers experienced problems: "About twenty passengers arrive daily from Boreas. As the coach frequently arrives on less than four wheels, many footmen are seen dragging their weary feet into town at the close of the day . . ." (*Rocky Mountain News*, June 3, 1882)

On April 7, 1902, the U.S. Postal Service closed the Boreas office only to rescind the order on April 28, 1902. After the reopening, residents no longer had to travel to Breckenridge for their mail. On October 28, 1903, Albert M. Dow became postmaster. Frank Soper replaced him on August 18, 1904. On January 31, 1905, the U.S. Postal Service issued another order closing the office. Once again Boreas residents traveled to Breckenridge for their mail.

Figure 2-25. Entrance to the Post Office at Boreas Pass during the "Great Blockade" in 1899. (Courtesy Maureen Nicholls)

Figure 2-26. Postmark from Boreas, Colo., April 27, 1901. (*Colorado Postal Historian*, Volume 16, Number 1, August, 2000)

Fires, often caused by sparks from the smokestacks on the engines, damaged the snowsheds.

"Fire on Saturday night destroyed the stone shed, the snow shed and the telegraph station at Boreas pass. The loss to the South Park road [railroad] will exceed $10,000." (*The Aspen Daily Times*, November 16, 1898)

"Snow-Shed Burned
On Wednesday morning, one of the long snow-sheds over the C. & S. railway track on east side of Boreas pass burned down, which interfered with the free operation of trains for a day or two.

The burned shed was 1,000 feet long and of course the cross ties under the rails for that distance were also destroyed. The rails, too, were twisted out of shape, so that an entirely new track had to be built. The loss will figure up $8,000 at least." *(Summit County Journal,* December 5, 1903)

Snow, not fire, caused the biggest problems and the greatest drain on the railroad's finances.

"Snow in the Colorado Mountains
COMO, COLO. January 12—Snow began falling here at 10 o'clock yesterday morning, accompanied by a fierce, cold wind. All last night the storm raged furiously. Reports from Boreas pass are to the effect that snow had greatly delayed all trains." (*The Colorado Daily Chieftain*, Pueblo, January 13, 1893)

"The snow and wind has kept the D. L. and G., [Denver, Leadville & Gunnison] people busy keeping the High Line open this week. At one time there were eight trains snowed in on Boreas Pass." (*Fairplay Flume*, March 26, 1897)

Writers often marveled at the scenery and the snow as they crossed Boreas Pass:
"Over the South Park Railroad is the Land Beyond
What magic still clings to that world! . . . The ride from Como to

Leadville—seventy miles—is one grand panorama, something to keep the blood tingling in your veins. I really believe some of us were higher than ever we shall be again . . . It is a continual twist and turn, up, up, up and around, now to the right, now to the left, over a magnificent smooth track. We are near Boreas, over 11,000 feet high, and now we are in a snow storm. Everything looks dark and gloomy for a few minutes, and the cloud has passed and the sun shines warm and the view is perfectly sublime.

The railroad company has distributed snow-shed material at the most exposed parts on the road; so there will be no more trouble from snow blockages. Here we are at the top. A large stone engine house with a turntable inside, is ready for winter work. At every side track we pass along freight trains. We run into the telegraph office and hear the welcome click, click of the instrument which joins us with friends many miles away in one instant.

The brakeman examines the air brakes and toot, toot, we are off on the down grade . . ." (*The Idaho Springs News*, September 18, 1885)

During the Great Blockade of winter 1898-1899, no trains crossed Boreas Pass between February 6 and April 24, 1899, a total of 78 days. **Figures 2-27** and **2-28** show Boreas Pass during that period.

Chapter 2 Boreas Pass Station

Figure 2-27. Buildings on Boreas Pass Buried in Snow, 1899. (Courtesy Maureen Nicholls)

Figure 2-28. Boreas Pass Telegraph Station, Section House, Storehouse, and Ventilation Pipe, 1899. (Courtesy Maureen Nicholls)

Figure 2-29. Heading toward Breckenridge with Five Helper Engines, 1899. Note the stone engine house on the far left. (Courtesy Maureen Nicholls)

Figure 2-30. Rotary Snowplow, near Boreas Pass. (Courtesy Maureen Nicholls)

Figure 2-31. Rotary Snowplow removing Deep Snow near Boreas Pass. (Courtesy Maureen Nicholls)

A year after the Big Snow, the newspaper editor admonished the railroad:
"Some More Storms
Last Saturday's JOURNAL vouchsafed the prediction that the C. and S. railroad would be free from snow and open for traffic on that day between Como and Leadville—the territory covered by the snow-blockade. That prediction was made in good faith, and would undoubtedly have proved true, were it not for the fatal disability to the rotary snowplow, ascending the Boreas pass from the Como side on that date.

On the way to Denver for repairs the big whirling machine collided with a locomotive and further disables its vital parts, so that by the time repairs were completed the territory between Breckenridge and Como previously open for traffic was visited by another terrific northerner and blockaded for a period of three full days.

In the meantime the half dozen engines hemmed in between Boreas and Kokomo ran out of coal and all efforts to open the High Line were practically abandoned, awaiting the arrival of the new rotary, which did not arrive here till two o'clock yesterday morning, followed by all delayed passengers, mail and express for Breckenridge and Dillon and the Blue river country—north of here . . .

A POINTER—It takes a good and substantial road bed, first-class engines plenty of fuel a strong rotary plow to operate a railroad over the hazardous territory traversed by the High Line and without all these requites the management cannot expect to perform even fairly satisfactory service." (*Summit County Journal*, February 24, 1900)

Not only crewmen suffered. Merchants awaiting goods found their supply chain impacted by a wreck.
"Bad Wreck.
Early Sunday morning a very bad wreck occurred on Boreas pass, just east of the summit. An extra freight, of twelve loaded cars,

eastbound, got away from the train crew at Boreas, and started down the hill at a terrific speed. The conductor and one brakeman were left behind. Brakeman Mundy stayed with the train. When all hope of checking the speed of the train was exhausted, the engineer and fireman jumped from the engine and thus save their lives.

Between snow sheds 6 and 7 the whole train left the track and piled up all in a heap killing Mundy instantly. The engine ran into the bank and was very badly damaged. Most of the cars and contents were scattered over the side of the mountain. In the shape of salvage, a tramp stealing a ride, went through the thickest of the wreck and came out uninjured." (*Summit County Journal*, June 8, 1901)

When railroad men jumped from a runaway train to save their lives, they called it "joining the birds."

The railroad kept helper engines at Dickey to use when heavy loads required extra horsepower to climb to Boreas Pass or Climax in the Ten Mile Canyon. After this accident, the helper engine brought the coroner.

"Engineer Dan Williams Killed.
Early on Monday morning word was brought to town by Conductor G. W. Miller, of the four o'clock a.m. train, that there was a wreck of his train at Pittsburg switch, about four miles from town. Coroner Dr. Condon and a number of citizens left on the engine that returned to the scene of the wreck after it had gone to Dickey ahead of the wrecked train that it had been helper to over the range and from Boreas it went on to Dickey where the engineer was informed of the wreck.

On the return of the engine to town the coroner had a jury of six . . . summoned and they went on the 11:30 train and viewed the remains and wreck and heard the evidence of Conductor Miller and Brakemen C. J. Selby and S. S. Cheyney, whose testimony varied but little from the following statement:

The train was moving at a rate of from ten to thirteen miles an hour. The two brakemen were in the fifth car from the engine and heard and felt no jar or other collision, greater than the breaking apart of the train. Thinking that had happened they and the conductor went forward and found the engine tender and three cars in a wreck with the engine on its right side, lying flat and the left side engine going like lightning, letting the steam escape. The conductor and one of the brakemen stepped on the tender trucks and saw the fireman, Frank Young, coming out between the tank and trucks, badly scalded and bruised up. They assisted him to the passenger car and returned and going around the engine found that engineer Dan Williams had crawled out between the cab and tender, having been scalded from head to foot. He asked them to get him out of there as quickly as they could, which they did and getting him to the car as quickly as they could he only lived about two hours. His injuries covered his whole body.

The jury examined the track, there seemed to be no spreading or other thing wrong with the track and the witnesses said in their evidence that these accidents wholly unexplainable and apparently unavoidable will be as long as cars run on two tracks." (*Breckenridge Bulletin*, January 3, 1903)

Summer didn't always offer a reprieve from the storms and deep snow on Boreas Pass.

The Colorado & Southern had a passenger train snowbound yesterday on Boreas pass thereby breaking all past records for late snows heavy enough to block traffic. The snow was about 4 feet deep on the pass, and it had drifted into the cuts until the Leadville train was unable to push its way through. The snowplow was pressed into service, and the train was dug out after a few hours' delay. A snow of that magnitude at this season of the year is remarkable—Denver Times." (*Daily Sentinal*, Grand Junction, June 1, 1909)

Chapter 2 Boreas Pass Station

Figure 2-32. Snowshed west of Boreas Pass, 1900. (Courtesy Maureen Nicholls)

Figure 2-33. Engine No. 9 entering the Snowshed on Boreas Pass. (Courtesy Maureen Nicholls)

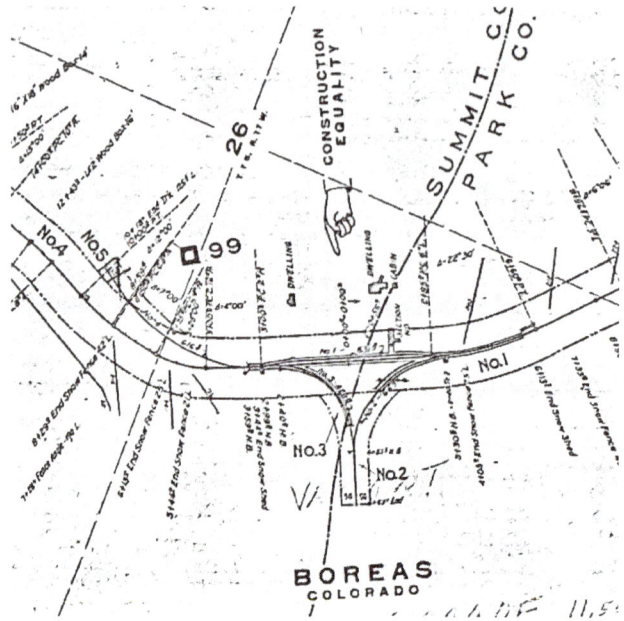

Figure 2-34. Portion of the Colorado & Southern Railway Map of Boreas Pass, 1918. The depot, section house, and wye remained but not the stone engine house. (Courtesy Bob Schoppe)

Figure 2-35. Dismantling Crew at Boreas Pass, August 28, 1938. The train consisted of bunk cars, a dining car, and a kitchen car. Snow fences still lined the tracks. (Courtesy Maureen Nicholls)

After 1938, the buildings on Boreas Pass deteriorated. Only the section house and storehouse remained by the 1960s.

In the late 1990s, the U.S. Forest Service restored the section house and wagon cabin, first using this smaller structure for wood storage. In 1998, the Forest Service, working with Summit Huts Association in Breckenridge, furnished the section house with facilities to welcome over-night visitors on a reservation basis. The wagon cabin now does the same.

Figure 2-36. Section House and Other Buildings, 1961. (Courtesy Maureen Nicholls)

Figure 2-37. Boreas Pass Section House, 1970s. (Courtesy Maureen Nicholls)

Figure 2-38. Section House and Stone Building, 1989. The 1918 ICC map identified the stone building on the left as a dwelling. Nothing remains of that building today. (Photograph by Author)

Figure 2-39. Section House, 1989. (Photograph by Author)

Figure 2-40. Boreas Pass Section House, 2021. (Photograph by Author)

Figure 2-41. The Lower Level of the Boreas Pass Section House, 2021. (Photograph by Author)

Figure 2-42. Ground Floor of the Boreas Pass Section House, 2021. (Photograph by Author)

Figure 2-43. Upper Floor of the Section House, 2021. (Photograph by Author)

Chapter 2 Boreas Pass Station

Figure 2-44. Panoramic View of Boreas Pass, 2021. The engine house would have been to the left. (Photograph by Author)

Figure 2-45. Aerial View of the Boreas Pass Section House. (Google Earth, Imagery ©2021 Maxar Technologies, U.S. Geological Survey, USDA Farm Service Agency, Map data ©2021)

CHAPTER 3
FARNHAM STATION

Site Location

Found along the Denver, South Park & Pacific line at milepost 100.0, 1.2 miles north of Boreas Pass, and exactly 10 miles south of Breckenridge, Farnham boasted a switching track or siding 480 feet long where trains coming from opposing directions could pass one another. The railroad completed this section of the "High Line" in 1882. The town, founded in 1881 and named for William H. Farnham, had a general store, large hotel/boardinghouse, and a post office.

Figure 3-1. Train at Farnham Station heading toward Boreas Pass, 1884. Note the station house in the distance on the right and the siding in the foreground. (Denver, South Park & Pacific Historical Society Collection)

Chapter 3 Farnham Station

Figure 3-2. Same View as Figure 3-1, 2022. (Photograph by Author)

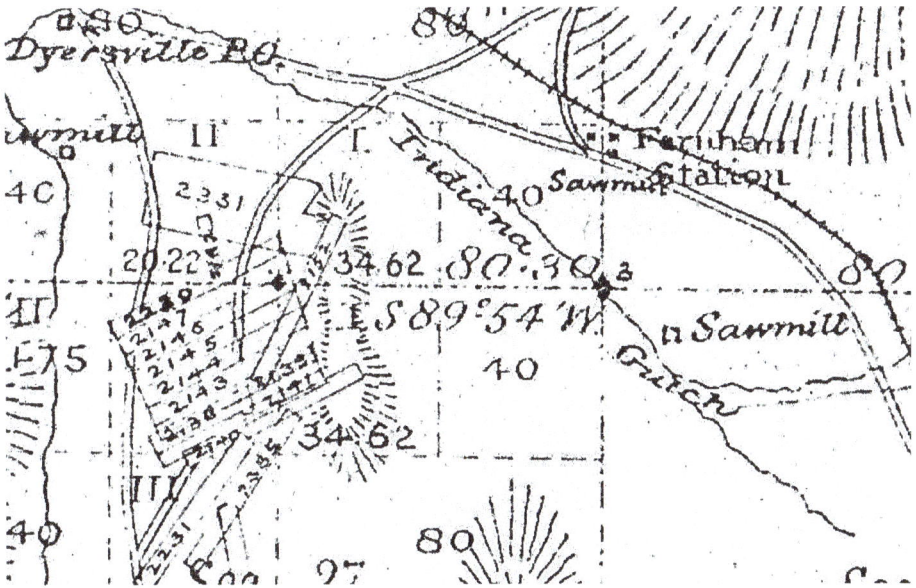

Figure 3-3. Portion of July 15, 1882, USGS Map showing Farnham. The double line indicates the stage road; the line with the cross cuts denotes the railroad track. Farnham had three buildings at that time. (Author's Collection)

The Town Itself

Daugherty told the story:

"Farnham was a station and post office exactly 100 miles from Denver on the Denver, South Park and Pacific Rail line. Located in the McBarnes Mining District, Farnham had a 480-foot switch track recently installed, and preparations were under way to make it a resort area. W.H. Farnham was the founder, promoter and postmaster of Farnham.

An article later appeared titled, 'Farnham, a New Mining Town in Summit County.' The article was actually a promotional letter signed by J. B. Farnham. Farnham was situated in an open park on the west slope of Bald Mountain, about one mile from the Continental Divide. The vista was said to be a superb one of the surrounding mountains, such as Bald, Bross, Lincoln, Hoosier, Silverheels, and Pacific. According to the article, a 'spacious' 16-room summer resort was being finished. It had a large parlor and dining hall, and large porches. The grounds were to be developed into a park with an area for croquet, promenades, and fountains, all to be situated near a small lake.

Farnham had a [general] store operated by Wilber F. Wood and Calvin H. Pike, with reportedly moderate prices . . .

The Colorado Business Directory listed Farnham from 1884 through 1898. From 1884 through 1886, the Shippers Guide section located Farnham on the stage road between Como and Breckenridge. From 1884 through 1896, Farnham was listed under business classifications by town. The village was on the Denver, South Park and Pacific Railroad, and had a population of 50 in 1884. The population increased to between 75 and 100 around 1890. In 1893 the population decreased to 35, which remained a constant until 1897, when the population was no longer listed.

Chapter 3 Farnham Station

From [December 2] 1881 through [November 2] 1895, Farnham served as the post office for the area, which included Boreas, and probably Dyersville and Dwyer. A general store was operated by W. F. Wood from 1883 to 1892, when C. H. Pike took over the ownership. The Warriors Mark Stamp Mill (15 stamps), which was close to Dyersville, was listed from 1889 through 1896. The 7-40 Consolidated Mining Company was listed from 1893 through 1896.

W.H. Farnham was the founder of the village bearing his name, in 1881. Previously he had been a resident of Denver and proprietor of the Denver Daily Hotel Reporter at 334 ½ Larimer Street. Farnham and his wife promoted the village as a resort, the wife designing the building. The circumstances of Mrs. Farnham's death, probably in 1883, and place of burial are unknown. I question whether Farnham's resort hotel was ever completed, for no reference was made in later sources to such an establishment. If the structure were completed, it probably served as a boarding house for miners working in the vicinity. Farnham occupied himself as the postmaster and mine owner in 1884. Farnham then disappeared for three years, and returned to the village in 1888. He served as justice of the peace until 1892, when he evidently left Farnham for good. A Mr. Farnham of the Leadville News-Reporter turned up in Breckenridge on business in 1900. This Farnham may have been W. H. Farnham because of Farnham's previous journalism experience in Denver.

Another long-time, prominent resident of Farnham was Calvin H. Pike. Pike opened a general store with W. [Wilbur] Wood about 1883, but must have sold out to Wood, as he turned up in 1884 as the postmaster of Golddale in Douglas County. Pike returned to Farnham in 1885, and became postmaster until 1896. Pike was a diversified individual, for besides being Farnham's postmaster, he was a mine owner, and railway ticket and express agent, ran W. Wood's store and acquired it in 1892, and was the local agent for the 7-30 mine for two years. In 1898, Pike's dwelling at Farnham was destroyed by fire. The cause was thought to be hot cinders from a passing train. Pike probably had a lumber contract in 1899, for he advertised for labor to work and cut timber. His post office address was listed as Boreas by this time.

Other Farnham residents mentioned in the Directories were W. Wood, J. S. Dowling, J. R. Muldoon, Henry Boaber, and John Mix.

Farnham was a stop through 1906 at least. Its station number was 1134 at one time and 552 in 1902. According to Poor, Farnham was also known as Flounders after the turn of the century..."

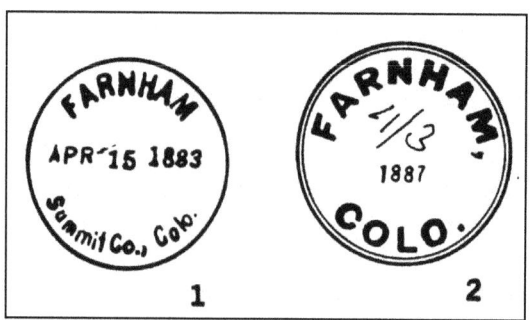

Figure 3-4. Postmarks of Farnham, April 15, 1883, and 1897. (*Colorado Postal Historian*, Volume 16, Number 1, August, 2000)

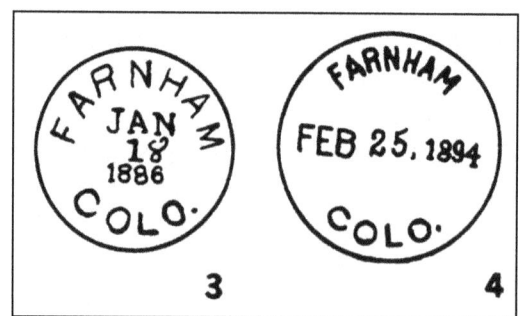

Figure 3-5. Postmarks of Farnham, January 18, 1886, and February 25, 1894. (*Colorado Postal Historian*, Volume 16, Number 1, August, 2000)

Figure 3-6. Postcard mailed from Farnham, 1886. (Courtesy Jerry Eggleston)

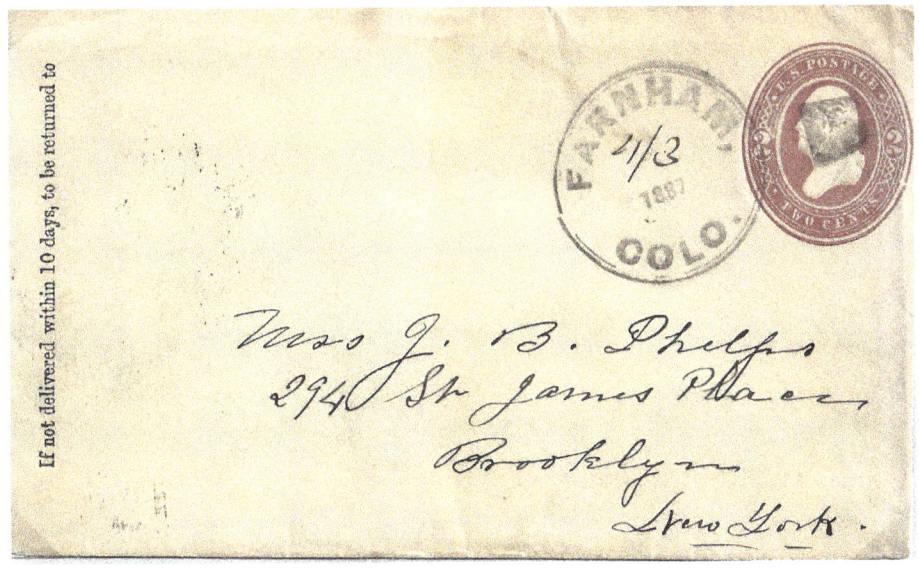

Figure 3-7. Postcard mailed from Farnham, 1887. (Courtesy Jerry Eggleston)

Figure 3-8. Farnham Station Site, looking Southwest. Residents of Dyersville and those working in the Warrior's Mark mine, located in the valley below, used this station for mail and rail service. (Courtesy Maureen Nicholls)

Figure 3-9. Same View as Figure 3-8, 2022. (Photograph by Author)

Chapter 3 Farnham Station

Figure 3-10. Looking West toward the Ten Mile Range, circa 1900. Electric poles lined the southern side of the railroad tracks. Farnham could be found to the right of the tracks in this photograph. (Courtesy Maureen Nicholls)

Figure 3-11. Same View as Figure 3-10, 2022. (Photograph by Author)

Figure 3-12. Looking West toward the Ten Mile Range. Snow fences helped keep heavy snow from burying the tracks near Farnham. (Courtesy Maureen Nicholls)

Figure 3-13. Similar View as Figure 3-12, 2022. (Photograph by Author)

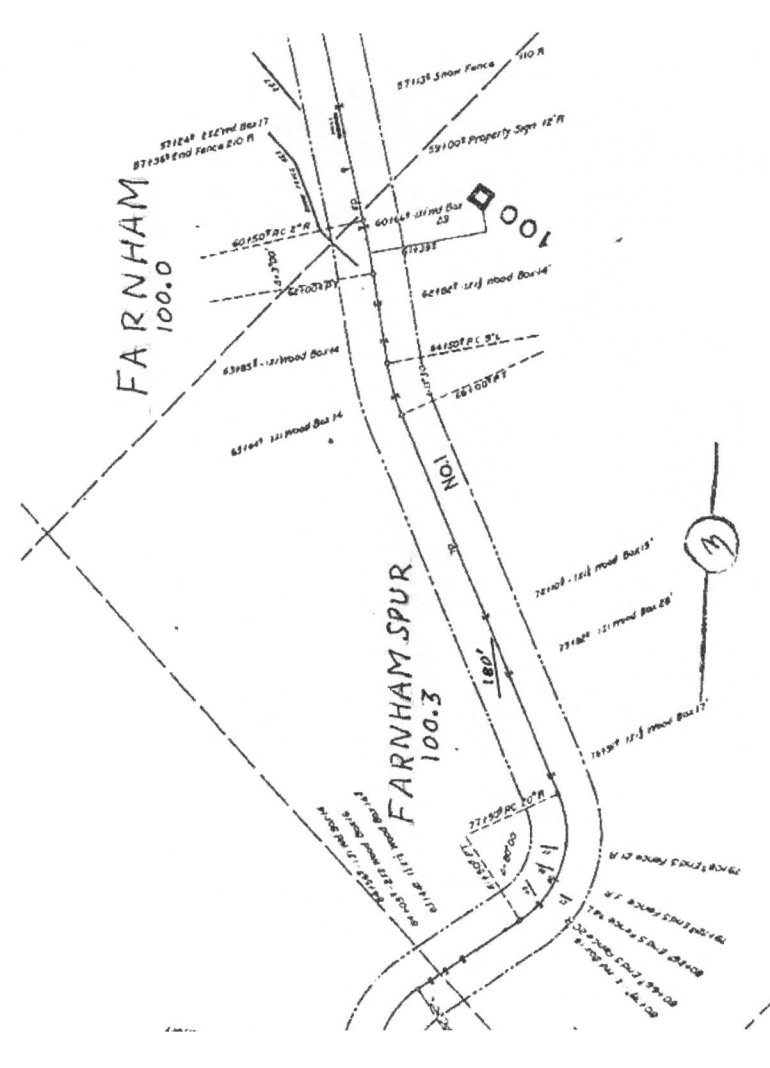

Figure 3-14. Colorado & Southern Map, including Farnham and Farnham Spur, located three-tenths of a mile west of Farnham, 1918. (Denver, South Park & Pacific Historical Society Collection)

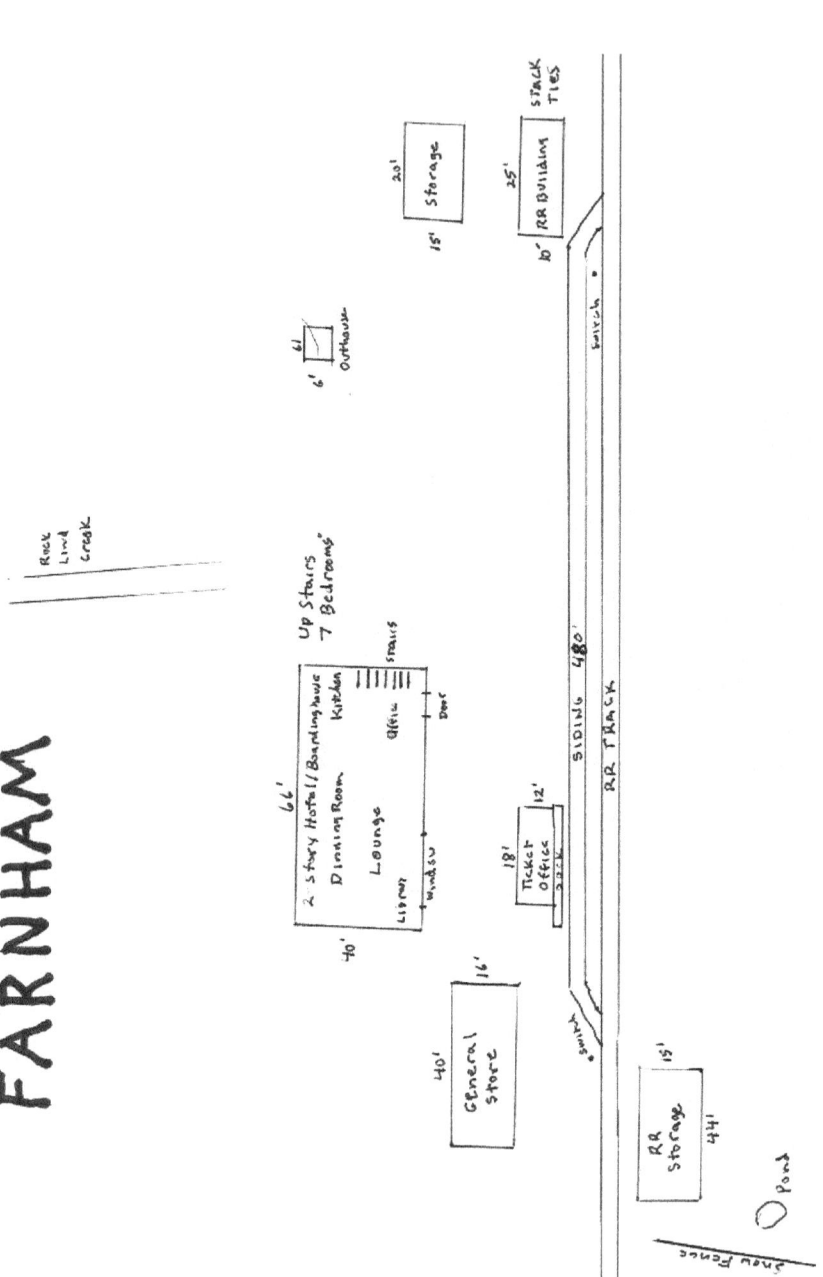

Figure 3-15. Hand-Drawn Map of Suggested Structures in Farnham in the late 1890s. (Drawn by Fountain and Rich Skovlin)

Farnham, 2022

Nothing remains of Farnham today except the footprints of some buildings surrounded by pieces of glass, pottery, cans, and other artifacts. On the south side of Boreas Road, near the structural remains, electrical wires lay on the ground. In **Figures 3-10** and **3-12**, electrical poles lined the tracks.

Figure 3-16. Electrical Wire on the Southern Side of Boreas Pass Road, 2022. (Photograph by Author)

Figure 3-17. Farnham Townsite, 2022. (Photograph by Author)

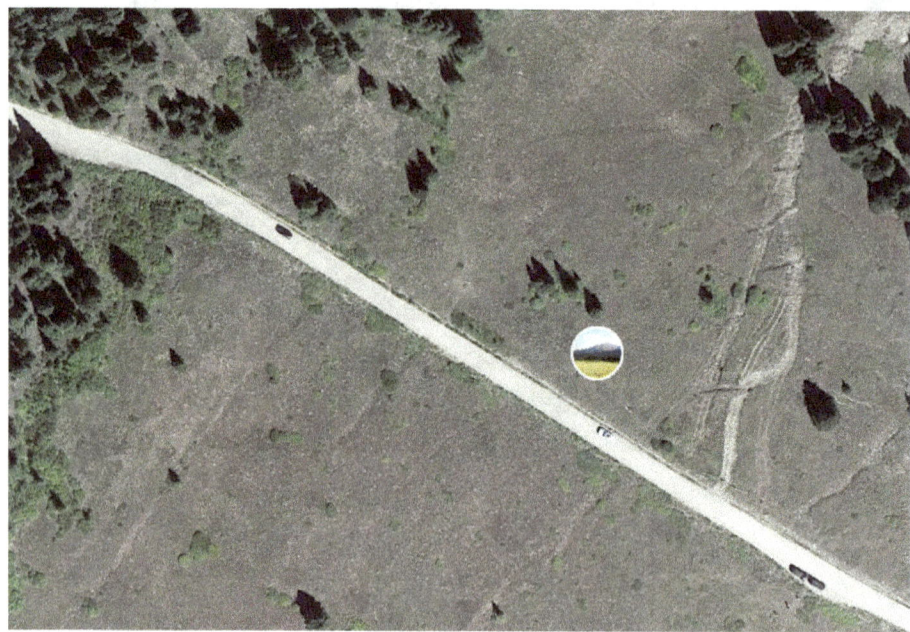

Figure 3-18. Aerial View of Farnham Townsite. (Google Earth, Imagery ©2021 Maxar Technologies, U.S. Geological Survey, USDA Farm Service Agency, Map data ©2021)

CHAPTER 4
FARNHAM SPUR

Site Location

Farnham Spur, located at milepost 100.03, three-tenths of a mile from Farnham Station on the Denver, South Park & Pacific line, had a 180-foot-long spur to serve the nearby 7-30 mining camp and surrounding timber-cutting operations.

7-30 Mine

Joseph J. Hostettler et al. filed Mineral Survey (MS) No. 2222, Silver Queen Lode on August 4, 1882. At the time of the survey, the claim included two shafts at the upper end of the claim.

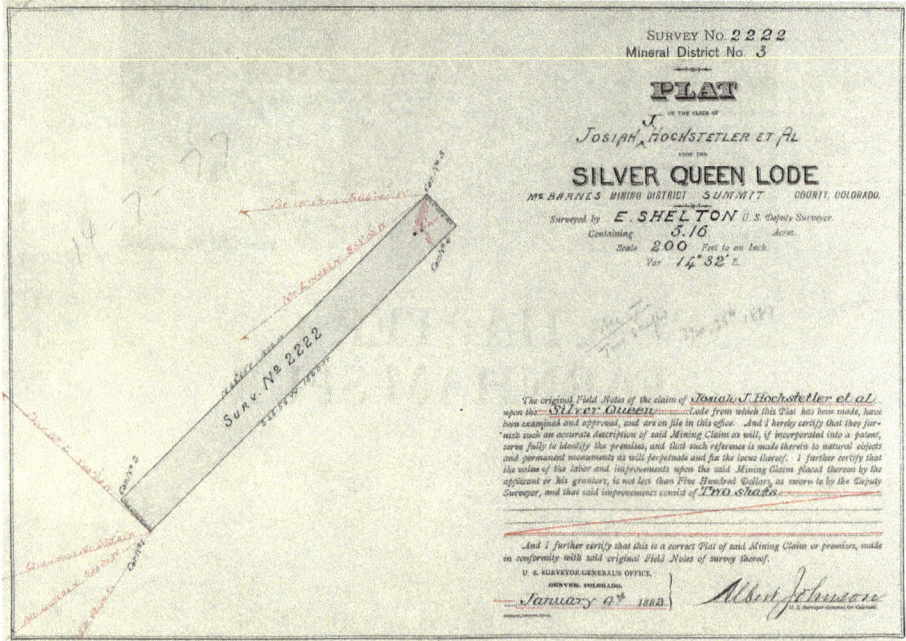

Figure 4-1. Mineral Survey (MS) No. 2222, Silver Queen Lode, filed on August 4, 1882. (Courtesy Bureau of Land Management)

The 7-30 mine on the steep eastern face of Bald Mountain, northeast of Farnham Spur, received its name because most workers began their day at 7:30 a.m. In 1883, William H. Iliff and Company, which included Joseph J. Hostettler, built a large boardinghouse with a separate building for a kitchen and dining room at the Farnham spur. Employees built one of the longest trams in Summit County extending from the spur to the 7-30 mine. A shaft house plus several other buildings surrounded the mine entrance.

The miners, who slept in the boardinghouse and ate in the dining room, rode the tram to and from the mine each day. The ride could be dangerous; whenever a bucket passed by a tower, the miners ducked to prevent being hit by the tower.

On March 30, 1889, Hostettler et al. filed Mineral Survey (MS) No. 5578, Seven-Thirty Lode, directly uphill from the Silver Queen. The surveyor noted several drifts and cross-cuts at the lower end of the claim.

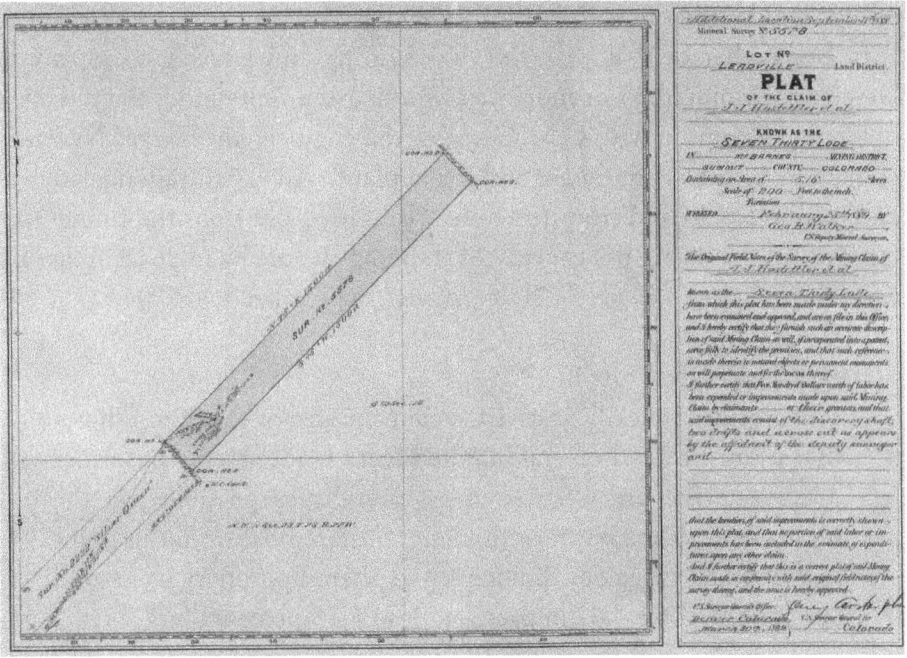

Figure 4-2. Mineral Survey (MS) No. 5578, 7-30 Lode. The lode claim extended uphill on Bald Mountain and included several drifts and cross-cuts. (Courtesy Bureau of Land Management)

Over the years, articles and references to this mine began calling it the 7-40 instead of the 7-30. Perhaps the confusion arose because the 7-40 Consolidated Mining Company, with H.F. Halleck, president, and C.H. Pike, local agent, owned the mine between 1893 and 1896. But then it could also be that the miners arrived late and didn't begin working until 7:40. Historical documents do not support this idea, though.

The 1920s

After years of little activity at the 7-30, the owners in 1922, the Alpha Mines Company, suspended its operations at their Warrior's Mark mine located down slope in Indiana Gulch and concentrated on the 7-30. By January, 1923, six men had driven a tunnel, expecting to encounter the vein within 30 feet. They hoped the new tunnel would cut the vein 300 feet deeper than the old tunnel higher on the mountain, which supposedly had a 20-inch streak of high-grade lead ore with both silver and gold.

In September of that year, the Aco Mining and Leasing Company of New York employed 35 or more men working the 7-30 under the direction of George Robinson with C.M. Glasgow the engineer-in-charge. New machinery included a compressor and steam plant. An aerial tram hauled men and equipment to and from the mine. It carried ore from the tunnel to a railroad siding, saving the expense of shipping the ore by mule train down a very steep incline. (*Summit County Journal*, September 1, 1923)

Berger and Sayre wrote in 1923:
"The lower tunnel . . . is caved . . . but the size of the dump shows that it must extend several hundred feet. Undoubtedly in former operations the ore was sorted as carefully as possible and the high-grade picked out for shipment. Surface float from this point showing quartz, galena, limonite, and altered porphyry went gold 0.16 ounce, silver 4.92 ounces, and lead 8.75 percent . . .

The upper Welch tunnel is said to be two or three hundred feet long but is only accessible for the first 50 feet. Here, representative samples of the best ore on the dump ran gold 0.18 ounce, silver

18.16 ounces, and lead 55.80 percent, or a total value of around $55 a ton. In the tunnel there is only one place where the main vein is accessible on account of close timbering. About 15 feet from the mouth a streak 8 to 10 inches wide and exposed for 5 or 6 feet in length ran gold 0.08 ounce, silver 17.82 ounces, and lead 34.40 percent, or approximately $40 a ton. Much of the float occurs in pieces which would indicate a vein several feet wide so that the width of the samples taken from the upper tunnels would not seem a fair representation of the average mining width. Many of the boulders of float consisting of nearly pure lead and lead carbonate are so big that a man could not lift them.

Above the upper Welch tunnel several open cuts and pits show ore continuing up towards the ridge, although the surface is soon covered with deep wash which gives no indication of the upper limit of the ore shoot.

The 30-foot shaft (Gold shaft) in porphyry near the middle of the Silver Queen claim is the next opening below the vein. Here again the dump is filled with honeycomb float, but apparently the character of the ore has changed largely to an auriferous [gold-bearing] pyrite. A sample of this float ran gold 2.60 ounce, silver 1.90 ounce, lead 1.25 percent, or a value of $52 a ton in gold. Another sample went gold 0.44 ounce, silver 1.06 ounce, that showed very little value.

The lower Rogers tunnel was cleaned out a year or two ago by Sauers, the present superintendent, and he states that the ore averages $110 a ton in gold, silver, and lead."

The South Park Zephyr

In 1937, Colorado & Southern abandoned the High Line. Before employees removed the tracks in the summer of 1938, John Riedesel modified a passenger automobile to run on the abandoned Colorado & Southern tracks:

"Clair and Gene Duggen had a good Model T Ford with a box on the back similar to a pickup, and we decided to use it for the project. Looking around for suitable wheels, we came up with some from an old section trailer or car, and their bolt pattern would fit the Model T hub. The major problem was to narrow the Model T tread width to the narrow-gauge thirty-six inches of the C&S track. Adapting the front axle was no problem; we just cut out part of the axle and welded it back together. The rear axle posed a bigger problem because we didn't have a lathe and couldn't afford to have the work done.

Searching an old junk yard we found some cluster gears from a Model B Ford transmission. They were ten inches long, and there were two of them in the junk pile. Welding the Model T outer wheel flanges to one end of the cluster gears made a good spacer, with the large end next to the wheel. The center axle housings were cut out ten inches, and the out and inner sections were welded back together, moving the outer axle bearings in on each side. The Model T axles are machined where the bearings normally run, but not their entire length. Since the major part of the axle is, therefore, larger in diameter (and rough), we couldn't fit the axle roller bearings in place. Not to worry! We removed the outer bearing sleeve in the axle housing and now had sufficient clearance. We knew this procedure was not totally proper but we didn't have the funds to do anything else. By greasing the bearings often they didn't give us any trouble. We cut the end from the rear springs and brazed the spring eye back under the mail leaf.

The front spring leaves were reversed putting the shorter leaves under the larger ones, and the assembly then remounted upside-down. The spring perches were also reversed, and the shackles installed over the perches. We brazed a stop on one side of the spring to hold things in line, and also made a setup to keep the wheels from turning. By removing a pin we could unlock the steering so the car could be driven on the street or turned around for the return trip on the railroad tracks.

Mechanically it never gave us any trouble. It would pull the passes in high gear. One of our first trips was over Kenosha Pass (10,000 feet), past Bailey, Colorado, to a siding. The brakes were the worst problem. If used too heavily the wheels would slide like being on ice, and one rear wheel would spin backwards. We only drove about twenty miles per hour so it wouldn't work the motor too hard.

To go to Fairplay, Colorado, which was ten miles away, we went south to Garo Junction, then north to Fairplay, and on to Alma mines. We could not go over Boreas Pass until late spring or early summer. We couldn't get to Leadville because the Climax Mine tailings had covered the tracks. After the snow had melted we went to Keystone. We made a lot of trips over Boreas Pass (11,422') and Breckenridge . . ."

Figure 4-3. The South Park Zephyr at Farnham Spur, 1938. Part of the large 7-30 boardinghouse can be seen on the right, to the rear. (Denver, South Park & Pacific Historical Society Collection)

Figure 4-4. Stuck in the Snow, 1938. The South Park Zephyr sometimes faced difficult conditions on its way to Boreas Pass. (Denver, South Park & Pacific Historical Society Collection)

USGS Report

In the 1951 USGS Bulletin 970, Quentin D. Singewald repeated the information about the tram carrying ore to Farnham station. He also noted that the tramway had collapsed by the time the railroad abandoned the line in 1938. He provided details:

"... The location of several cabins, partly collapsed, at the head of the former aerial tramway are shown approximately on the 12,250-foot contour of plate 1. An adit driven from the southernmost cabin did not expose a vein. In a ravine northeast of the cabins, and at higher altitudes, are five adits along the Seven-Thirty vein, all of which disclosed ore ... a map of the Seven-Thirty workings made by H. J. Jay, Jr., deceased, and furnished by George Robinson.

The Evans adit is the lowermost and the Welch adit the uppermost of the five adits shown along the Seven-Thirty vein on Plate 2 (**Figure 4-6**). One adit now located between the Seymour and Rogers adits apparently had not been driven when Jay mapped the mine. The June adit of Jay's map did not disclose any ore and is not plotted on plates 1 or 2.

Shipments from the Seven-Thirty mine, according to George Robinson, were mainly of lead ore, and their aggregate value amounted to about $60,000. As shown on plate 1 the vein is either in or closely associated with a large fault transverse to the Boreas Pass major longitudinal fault. The Seven-Thirty fault probably continues more than a mile southwestward to the Warrior's Mark properties. It displaces all the sedimentary strata and the huge mass of monzonite porphyry capping Bald Mountain . . ."

Figure 4-5. Map showing the Seven-Thirty (7-30) Mine, 1940. By then, Farnham no longer appeared on maps. This map includes the abandoned railroad line from Boreas Pass to Bakers tank as well as the train station of Belmont. (*Geology and Ore Deposits of the Upper Blue River Area, Summit County, Colorado.* Geological Survey Bulletin 970, 1951)

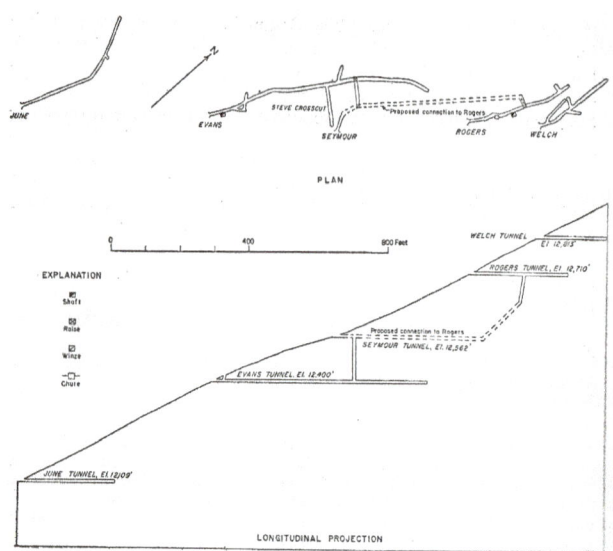

Figure 4-6. Underground Tunnel System of the Seven-Thirty (7-30) Mine, 1940. (*Geology and Ore Deposits of the Upper Blue River Area, Summit County, Colorado.* Geological Survey Bulletin 970, 1951)

The 7-30 in the 1970s

Figure 4-7. The Seven-Thirty (7-30) Shaft House and Tram House, Elevation over 12,000 Feet, 1975. Two tram towers lead down the mountain. (Courtesy of the Summit Historical Society)

Figure 4-8. Side View of the Seven-Thirty (7-30) Tram House, 1975. (Courtesy of the Summit Historical Society)

Figure 4-9. Lower Tram Tower of the 7-30 Mine, July 9, 2020. (Courtesy C.J. Mueller)

Figure 4-10. Lower Tram Tower of the 7-30 Mine, August 3, 2022. The tower had collapsed as early as 2021. (Courtesy C.J. Mueller)

Figure 4-11. Highest Tram Tower of the 7-30 Mine, August 3, 2022. By this time, wind and weather had caused the collapse of this tower, also. (Courtesy C.J. Mueller)

Figure 4-12. The Seven-Thirty (7-30) Mine Dumps, 2021. Note the building near the dumps and the remains of the lower tram tower in the foreground on the left. (Photograph by Author)

Figure 4-13. Close-up of a Building near the Adits of the Seven-Thirty (7-30) Mine. (Photograph by Author)

Figure 4-14. Aerial View of Farnham (lower, left) and the 7-30 Mine. Note the small, rust-colored dump of the 7-30 mine in the upper, right corner. (Google Earth, Imagery ©2021 Maxar Technologies, U.S. Geological Survey, USDA Farm Service Agency, Map data ©2021)

Farnham Spur and Mining Camp 1960s & 1970s

Figure 4-15. The Large Boardinghouse and Separate Structure containing the Kitchen and Dining Room, 1962. (Courtesy Maureen Nicholls)

Figure 4-16. Boardinghouse, 1960s. Workers used large, strong timbers to frame the building. (Courtesy Maureen Nicholls)

Figure 4-17. Boardinghouse, center; Kitchen/Dining Room, right rear; and Log Storage Building, right front. The smaller building with kitchen and dining room stood next to the boardinghouse. (Denver Public Library, Western History Department, X-3518)

Figure 4-18. Large Log Building used by the Railroad for Storage, 1960s. This 15-foot by 45-foot building stood farthest to the east. (Denver Public Library, Western History Department, X-5213)

Figure 4-19. Approaching Farnham from the East, 1975. The frame of the boardinghouse identifies the site. (Courtesy of the Summit Historical Society)

Figure 4-20. Boardinghouse, looking North, 1975. (Courtesy of the Summit Historical Society)

Figure 4-21. Boardinghouse, looking West, 1970s. (Courtesy of the Summit Historical Society)

Figure 4-22. Log Storage Building, 1975. The railroad constructed the 15-foot by 45-foot building, which sat farthest to the east in the camp. (See Figure 4-18.) (Courtesy of the Summit Historical Society)

Farnham Spur Today

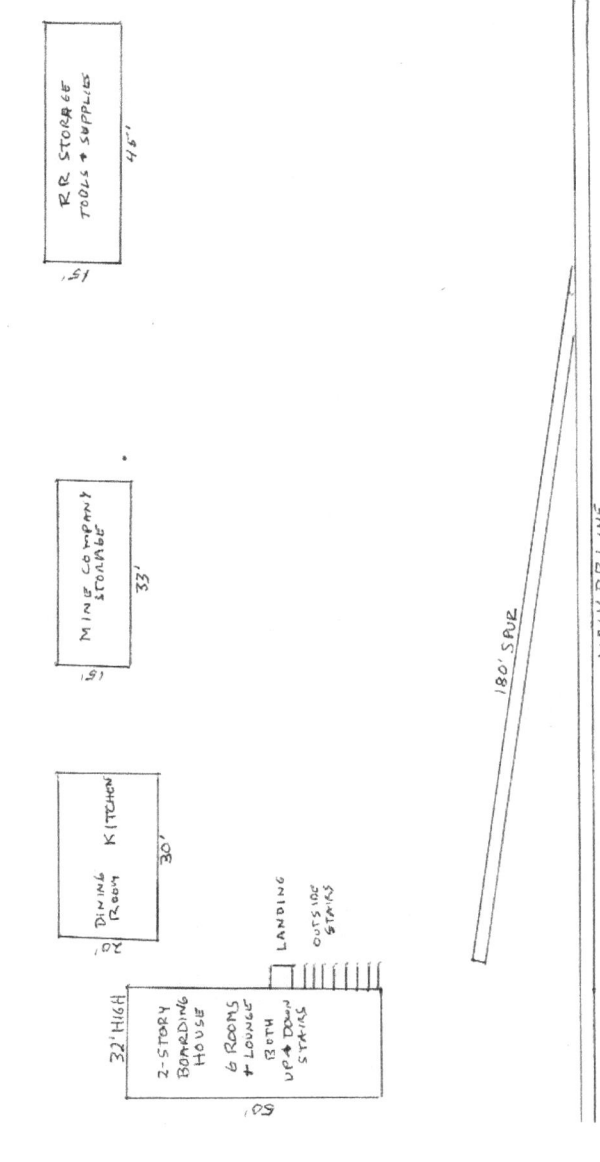

Figure 4-23. Hand-Drawn Map of Farnham Spur as it might have looked in the Late 1890s. Note the spelling of dinning. (Drawn by Fountain and Rich Skovlin)

Figure 4-24. Panoramic View of Farnham Spur Site, 2021. Only large timbers, logs, footprints of long-gone buildings, and the bed of the spur identify the site today. (Photograph by Author)

Figure 4-25. Collapsed Timbers of the Boardinghouse, 2021. (Photograph by Author)

Figure 4-26. Remains of the Kitchen and Dining Room, 2021. Compare to Figures 4-15, 4-17, 4-19, and 4-20. (Photograph by Author)

Figure 4-27. Site of the 15-Foot by 45-Foot Log Railroad Storage Building. Compare to Figures 4-18 and 4-22. (Photograph by Author)

Figure 4-28. Path of the Spur. (Photograph by Author)

Figure 4-29. Aerial View of the Farnham Spur Site. A few logs from the boardinghouse cover the ground in the upper, left section of the clearing. The remains of smaller buildings can be seen to the right of the boardinghouse site. (Google Earth, Imagery ©2021 Maxar Technologies, U.S. Geological Survey, USDA Farm Service Agency, Map data ©2021)

CHAPTER 5
DWYER/BELMONT STATION

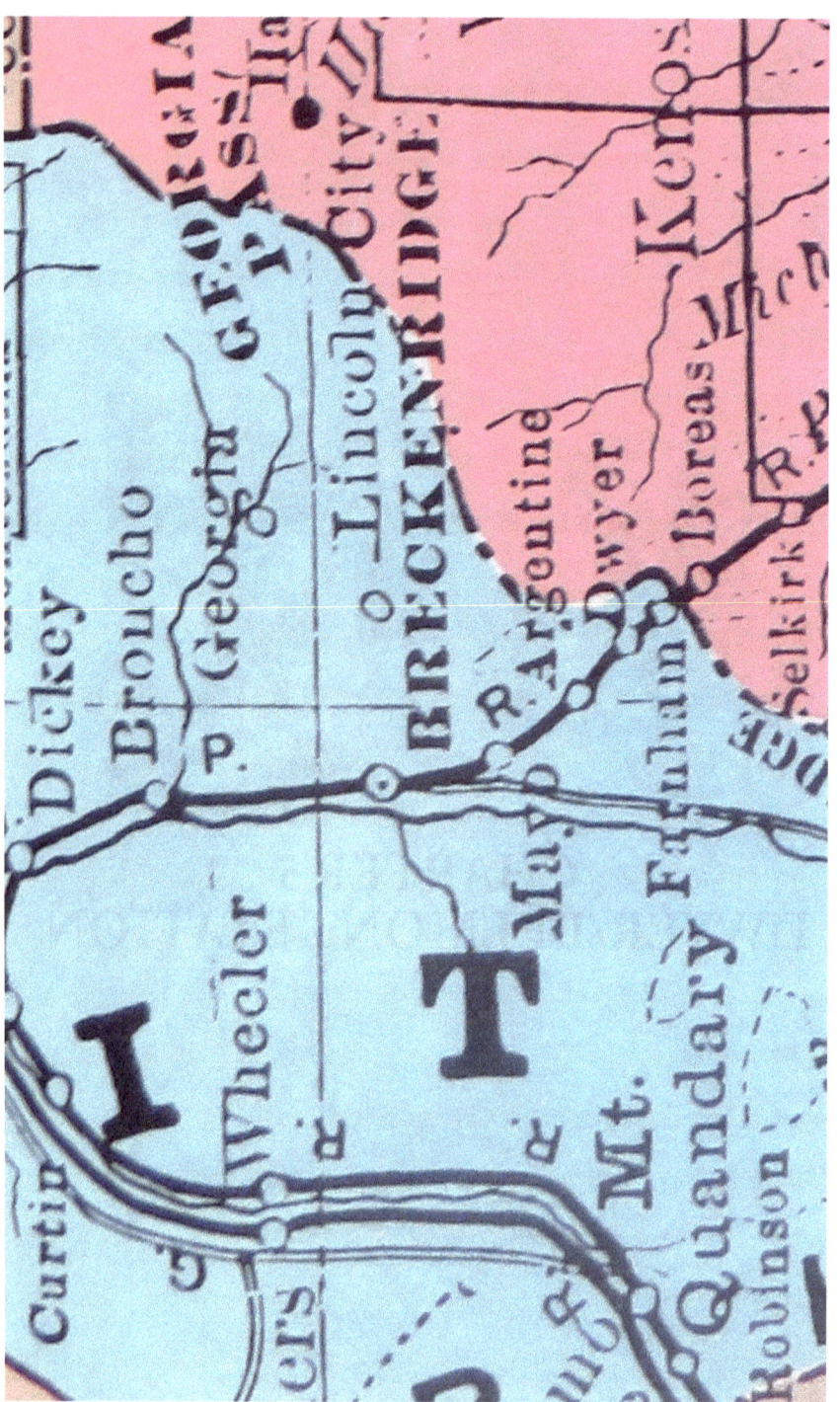

Figure 5-1. Portion of Crofutt's 1885 Map showing Dwyer. (*Grip Sack Guide to Colorado*)

Site Location

Dwyer/Belmont, train station No. 1135 with a 738' spur located at elevation 11,104' on the DSP&P line at milepost 100.80, two miles north of Boreas Pass and nine miles south of Breckenridge, served nearby mines.

Figure 5-2. Train Wreck near Dwyer Spur, 1898. (Courtesy Maureen Nicholls)

Little information exists to tell the story of Dwyer. A July 15, 1882, USGS map drawn by Harvey Fry does not include Dwyer; instead, the map identifies Farnham Station, about three quarters of a mile to the east of Dwyer's location. Because Dwyer appears on the 1885 map, a founding date between 1882 and 1885 can be assumed. (**Figure 5-1**)

Mining Claims

Thomas West and partners located the Sunny Side lode claim in the McBarnes Mining District on August 27, 1886. George B. Walker surveyed the claim measuring 5.16 acres (150' x 1500') on June 22, 1895. The owners received Mineral Survey (MS) No. 9580 on September 5, 1895.

They located the Balsome lode claim on October 14, 1887, and the Handy lode claim on January 3, 1888, both in the McBarnes Mining District. Walker surveyed the two claims totaling 10.32 acres (each 150' by 1,500') on July 17, 1895. The government issued Mineral Survey (MS) No. 9575 on September 5, 1895.

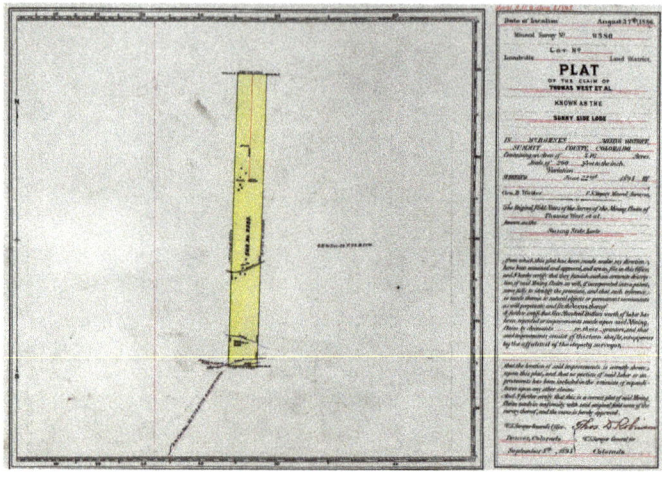

Figure 5-3. Mineral Survey (MS) No. 9580, Sunny Side Lode, September 5, 1895. (Courtesy Bureau of Land Management)

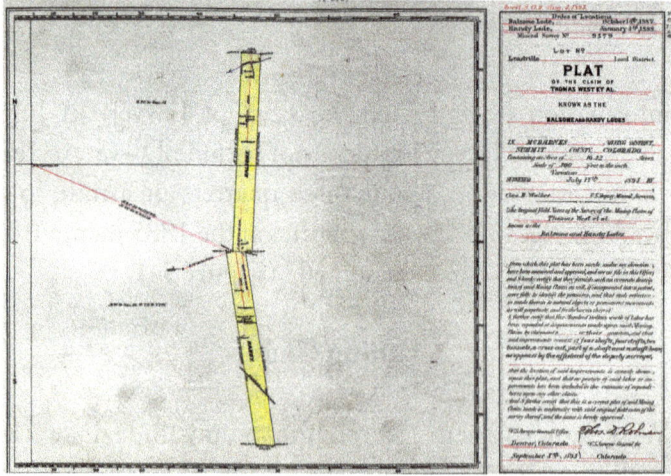

Figure 5-4. Mineral Survey (MS) No. 9579, Balsome and Handy Lodes, September 5, 1895. (Courtesy Bureau of Land Management)

Chapter 5 Dwyer/Belmont Station

The Sunny Side lode (**Figure 5-3**), in the town of Dyersville, crosses Indiana Creek. The lode map includes a house between the creek and nearby ditch. Dwyer could be found a short distance from this claim.

The Denver, Leadville & Gunnison tracks cut across the Handy Lode. (**Figure 5-4**) About 300 feet directly up the hill, to the north, where the spur meets the main track, two shafts, a shaft house, a cross cut, and a blacksmith shop can be seen. **Figure 5-10** shows the blacksmith shop and the caved-in shaft appears in **Figure 5-11**.

Responding to prospecting and mining in the area, the Denver, South Park & Pacific established a station at Dwyer, gave it number 1135, and built a 738-foot-long spur for loading ore that connected on the east end to the main line.

The railroad built only a station house. Remnants of cabins, mine dumps, and a large shaft give evidence that Dwyer functioned as a mining camp. No retail stores served the needs of the miners, requiring them to travel to Farnham for supplies and mail.

The 1886 Denver, South Park & Pacific map from Boreas summit to Breckenridge drawn incorrectly by M.C. Poor in 1976 identified the station as Belmont. At that time, it still carried the name Dwyer, as it did in 1898.

Figure 5-5. Rotary Snowplow operating at Dwyer, circa 1900. (Courtesy Maureen Nicholls)

Name Change

After the turn of the century, Dwyer became Belmont, most likely the name of one of the railroad's executives at the time.

The *Summit County Journal* first used the name Belmont on July 22, 1916: "Miss Agnes Roby and her guest Miss Maude Leslie went to Belmont Thursday where they had a pleasant outing."

Because the station and its spur appeared on a 1918 Colorado & Southern map, the station probably remained active up to that point, but following the usual boom-to-bust cycle, the Balsome and Handy lodes (MS 9579) as well as the Sunny Side lode (MS 9580) appeared on the Summit County delinquent tax list in 1922. (**Figure 5-6**).

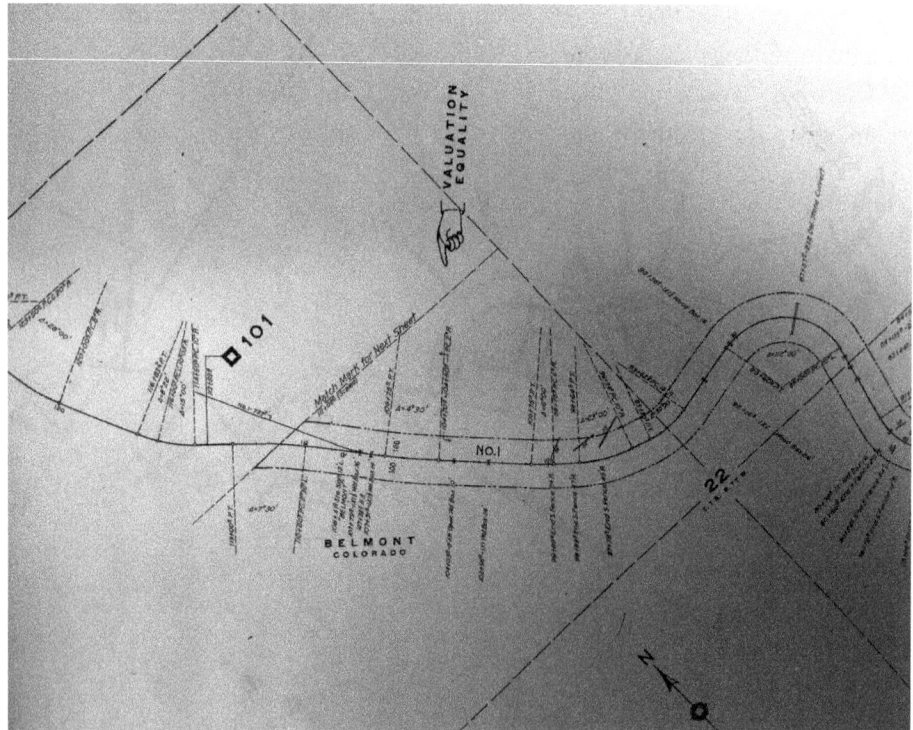

Figure 5-6. Railroad Map showing Belmont, 1918. A sign announced the name of the station. The diagonal line moving away from the tracks indicates the 723-foot-long spur. (Courtesy Bob Schoppe)

Chapter 5 Dwyer/Belmont Station

Dwyer Spur, 1930s

By the 1930s, miners had deserted the played-out mines in the area. The railroad probably removed the Dwyer spur rails prior to total abandonment of the line in 1937.

Figure 5-7. The Dwyer Spur, circa 1930s. The Dwyer spur (on the right) runs behind the snow-covered speeder and disappears in the trees. (Courtesy John Hallinan Collection)

Two speeders (**Figure 5-7**) sit on the main line (left) and on the spur (right). Speeders replaced the old handcars.

"The speeders from this era usually had the "hit and miss" type engines. They were heavy with 1 or 2 big heavy flywheels and didn't create a lot of power for their weight but were simple and reliable. These were rpm-controlled in that when they reached a certain (max) rpm, the ignition would shut off and they would "coast" for a bit with those heavy flywheels. When the rpm went down to a certain point, the ignition would turn on again and they would accelerate/rev up. Primitive but obviously a BIG improvement over handcars. Later, companies like Fairmont used more conventional 2- and 4-stroke engines." (Courtesy Bob Schoppe)

Long after its heyday, Belmont appeared on a 1940 map. (**Figure 4-5**) Does this mean that Belmont remained an active mining camp?

Mining Activity

Fountain, along with Rich Skovlin and Rick Hague, spent August 8, 2019, hiking the hillside above the Dwyer spur. They found numerous prospect pits or holes and several collapsed shafts; the corner stones of claims (**Figures 5-9, 5-10**); and a blacksmith shop, shaft, and remnants of the shaft house. (**Figures 5-11, 5-12**)

An over-grown but well-defined road led from the railroad spur uphill. (**Figure 5-14**) Fountain followed the road to a plateau at the southwest foot of Bald Mountain. (**Figure 5-15**) Here, it split; one branch headed toward Bald Mountain—the other led down slope. Both branches accessed area mines. Miners most likely used the road to transport ore to the Dwyer spur.

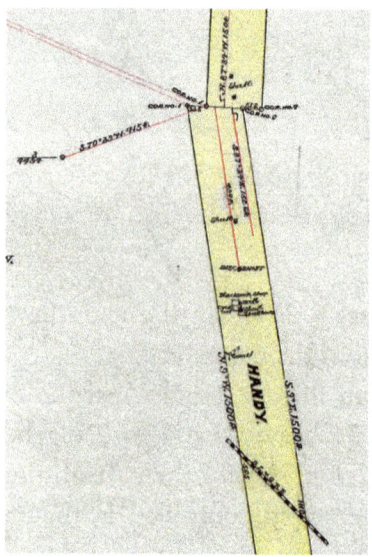

Figure 5-8. Portion of Mineral Survey (MS) No. 9579. The survey, drawn in 1895, includes Corner Stones No. 1 and No. 4 of the Balsome lode and Corner Stones No. 1 and 2 of the Handy lode; and the blacksmith shop, shaft, shaft house, and Denver, Leadville & Gunnison track. The DL&G replaced the bankrupt Denver, South Park & Pacific in 1889. (Bureau of Land Management)

Chapter 5 Dwyer/Belmont Station

Figure 5-9. Corner Stone No. 2 of the Handy Lode, refer to Figure 5-8, 2019. (Photograph by Author)

Figure 5-10. Corner Stone No. 4 of the Balsome Lode, refer to Figure 5-8, 2019. (Photograph by Author)

Figure 5-11. Blacksmith Shop on the Handy Lode, refer to Figure 5-8, 2019. (Photograph by Author)

Figure 5-12. Collapsed Shaft and Remnants of Shaft House on the Handy Lode, refer to Figure 5-8, 2019. The shaft measured about 138 feet deep. (Photograph by Author)

Figure 5-13. Tram Cable, 2019. About 1,000 feet of cable lays near the spur. Did the men intend to build a 500-foot-long tram to carry ore from the shaft to the spur? Refer to Figure 5-12 to see the shaft near the spur. (Photograph by Author)

Figure 5-14. Well-Defined Road leading Uphill from the Spur toward Bald Mountain. (Photograph by Author)

Figure 5-15. Uphill Access Road. The branching road provided easier access to the railroad spur. (Photograph by Author)

Thomas West, one of the original discoverers of the Sunny Side, Balsome, and Handy lodes, found success at the Hamilton mine in Summit Gulch in 1899 and the Germania mine on Little Mountain in 1902-1903. He made a trip to Denver on November 18, 1912, and died the next day at the Midland Hotel at the age of 50.

Chapter 5 Dwyer/Belmont Station

Dwyer and Dwyer Spur Today in Photographs

Figure 5-16. Panoramic View of Dwyer, from Boreas Pass Road, 2021. The grade for the 723-foot-long spur extends from left to right. Workers removed the rails many years ago; however a few rotten ties remain in place. (Photograph by Author)

Figure 5-17. Railroad Ties from the Spur. Railroad work crews removed the trackage in 1938 leaving just a few wooden ties to rot in place. (Photograph by Author)

Figure 5-18. Coal from Engines and Smokestacks. (Photograph by Author)

Figure 5-19. Remnants of a Cabin at Dwyer, 2019. (Photograph by Author)

Chapter 5 Dwyer/Belmont Station

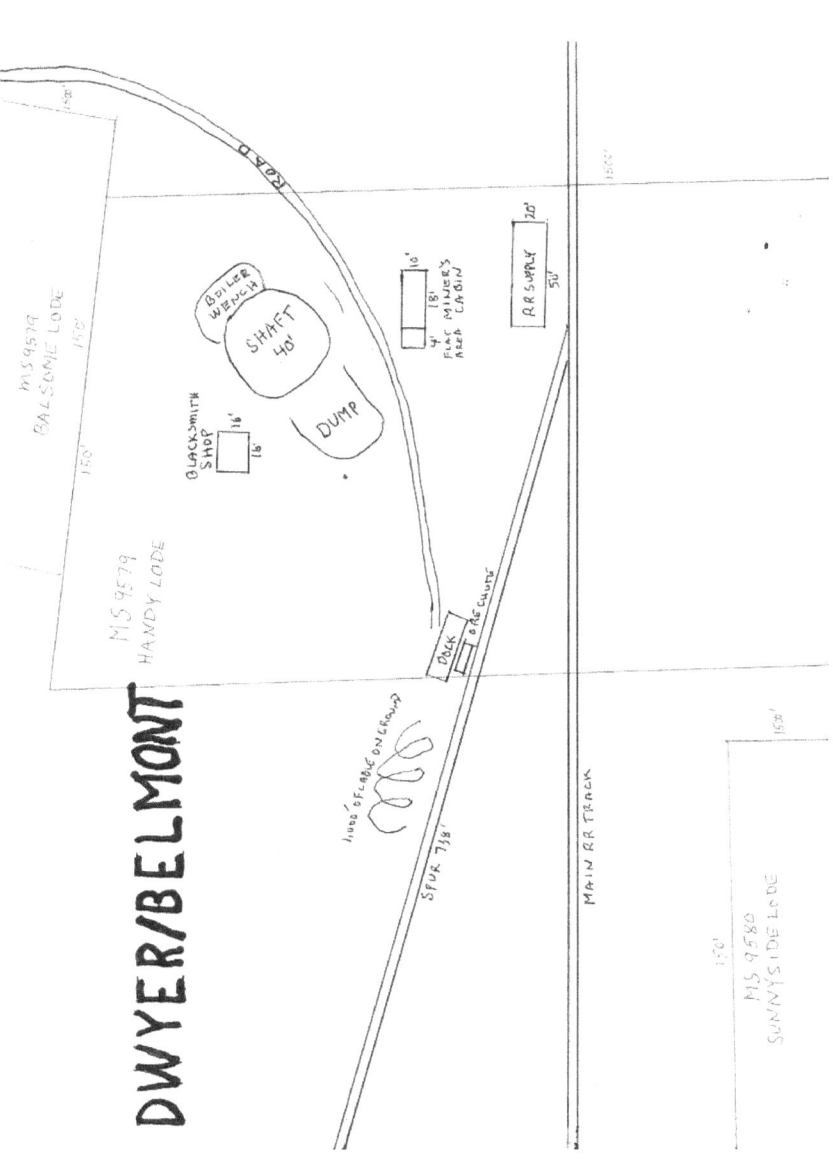

Figure 5-20. Hand-Drawn Map of Dwyer/Belmont. Fountain and friend, Rich Skovlin, used clues on the landscape to imagine how the settlement might have looked in the late 1890s. (By Author and Rich Skovlin)

Figure 5-21. Aerial View of the Dwyer/Belmont Location, 2021. The remnants of the blacksmith shop in Figure 5-11 can be seen in the upper, middle portion of the photograph. (Google Earth, Imagery ©2021 Maxar Technologies, U.S. Geological Survey, USDA Farm Service Agency, Map data ©2021)

CHAPTER 6
SIGNATURE SANDSTONE

While not an official train stop, Signature Sandstone, located 0.8 miles east of Bakers tank and 1.1 miles west of Dwyer/Belmont, became important because trains often stopped to allow passengers time to carve their names or initials and date in the red sandstone on the north side of the tracks.

Now that the old train route has become a popular route for travelers in the summer and a cross country ski route in the winter, people continue adding their names and initials in the sandstone, sometimes obliterating the old carvings.

Figures 6-2 through **6-5** show some of the oldest markings still visible.

Figure 6-1. Approaching Signature Sandstone from Boreas Pass, 2022. (Photograph by Author)

Chapter 6 Signature Sandstone

Figure 6-2. G.K. Smith, carved 1885. HANSEN BROS added their name a century later, in 1985. (Photograph by Author)

Figure 6-3. Visible Date, JUN 1891, but Unclear Signature. (Photograph by Author)

Figure 6-4. HARPER, added in 1926. (Photograph by Author)

Figure 6-5. F F E, signed in 1938. Could he have been part of the railroad's dismantling crew in 1938? (Photograph by Author)

Chapter 6 Signature Sandstone

Figure 6-6. Approaching Signature Sandstone from Breckenridge, 2022. (Photograph by Author)

CHAPTER 7
BAKERS TANK

Site Location

Bakers tank, elevation 10,871 feet, can be found at milepost 102.16 on the Denver, South Park & Pacific High Line, 3.32 miles from Boreas Pass and 7.84 miles from the Breckenridge station. The original tank dates from 1882 when the DSP&P built the line from Como to Dillon. The tank supplied water for the steam locomotives traveling along the route. (**Figure 1-3**)

Twitty explained: "Occasional mention in historic newspapers confirms that a tank and service station existed at today's site during the 1880s and 1890s, but the station's content remains unknown."

The name of the tank has been spelled several ways: Baker, Baker's, Bakers. Unless a direct quote, the name here will be Bakers.

By 1902, the Colorado & Southern had taken over the line and renamed the stop Station Number 554, milepost 102.0.

Figure 7-1. Colorado & Southern Rotary Snowplow clearing Track at the Original, Smaller Bakers Tank that held 9,305 Gallons of Water, Winter, 1899. Shovelers assist in the clearing process. (*Denver South Park & Pacific, Memorial Edition*, M.C. Poor)

Chapter 7 Bakers Tank

Figure 7-2. Denver, South Park & Pacific Engine taking on Water at Bakers Tank, circa 1900. A larger tank replaced the smaller tank in 1910. This mixed train pulled both freight and passenger cars. (Denver, South Park & Pacific Historical Society Collection)

The Mountain Pride Mine and Mill

Mountain Pride Mine and Mill, located nearby, used the 350-foot spur at Bakers tank to store empty railroad cars. By using the spur for storage, the company did not disrupt the trains using the main line.

The Mountain Pride group of claims consisted of the Waltham No. 2, Waltham No. 1, Williamsport, Mountain Pride, General Grant, Lincoln, and O.I.C. lodes. The oldest of the claims, the O.I.C. lode, has a location certificate date of July 1, 1886. Relocation certificates were filed on the Waltham No. 2, Waltham No. 1, Williamsport, Mountain Pride, General Grant, and Lincoln lodes on October 27, 1890. The Mountain Pride Gold Mining Company received Mineral Survey (MS) No. 6735 for all seven claims on December 31, 1890. (**Figure 7-3**) The survey shows one meandering tunnel about 700 feet long with several drifts leading away from it. The survey also includes a 40-foot-long tunnel, several shafts, a "trench," a house, a log house, and a cabin, all on the Williamsport and Mountain Pride claims.

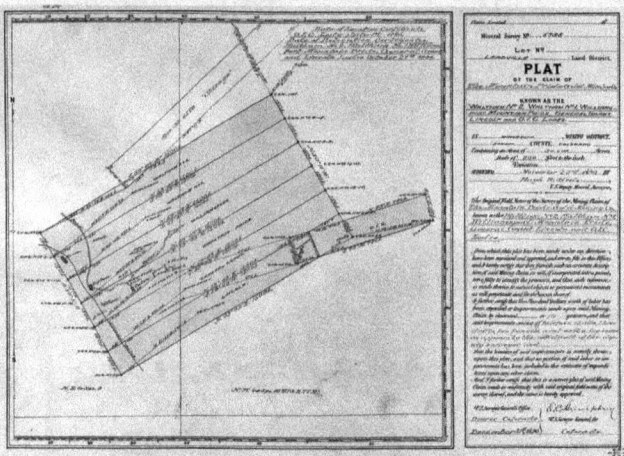

Figure 7-3. Mineral Survey (MS) No. 6735, Waltham No. 2, Waltham No. 1, Williamsport, Mountain Pride, General Grant, Lincoln, and O.I.C. Lodes, filed by The Mountain Pride Gold Mining Company, December 31, 1890.

Very little has been written about the early days of the Mountain Pride mine. Ransome felt that the mine began production around 1889. The *Summit County Journal* (March 2, 1895) noted that Dan McNiel shipped a carload of ore from the Mountain Pride the previous Monday. Two years later (December 18, 1897), the newspaper advised that "J. E. Jones, secretary and treasurer of the Mountain Pride Mining Co., arrived from St. Louis Wednesday and has been busy looking over the property of the company."

Two Deaths at the Mountain Pride

On March 2, 1898, a fire caused by an unattended candle at the Mountain Pride burned the bunkhouse and shaft house. Thomas Harvey, an Englishman, and M.T. Harvey, an unrelated American, suffocated from the smoke in the mine. Another miner, George Williams, escaped by climbing the emergency ladder.

Harry C. Foote, Superintendent

Possibly before May, 1898, Harry C. Foote became superintendent of the mine that the *Journal* called one of "the best appointed and most ably managed mines in the district." Miners worked three shifts of eight hours each, while the engineers, pumpmen, topmen, and blacksmiths worked 12-hour shifts. The mine employed a total of 25 men.

A 700-foot tunnel, 140 feet below the surface, cut the 500-foot-deep shaft. Miners dug five levels below the tunnel level but most work occurred on the fourth level. The steam drill, on the sixth or bottom level, drilled eight to ten five-foot exploratory holes each shift. The No. 9 and No. 7B Cameron pumps capable of pumping 150 gallons per minute operated on the lower level, also. Two 60-horsepower boilers and one 20-horsepower hoist provided power for the machinery on the property.

Figure 7-4. The Mountain Pride Mill and Cabins, circa 1898. (Courtesy Maureen Nicholls)

Diamond Drill

In the summer of 1898, Foote used a diamond drill to sink a 1,000-foot-deep exploratory hole. An on-site laboratory tested the samples recovered. By the end of August, the hole had reached a depth of 190 feet. At 280 feet, the drill found traces of copper and lead, but not much else. On October 1, the *Journal* reported that at a depth of 900 feet, "nothing of importance has been uncovered as yet." In mid-October, now down over 1,000 feet, the effort still had produced little of value. In the previous 10 years, the company had invested over $100,000 in the Mountain Pride property.

While the exploratory hole found no ore of value, levels 4 and 5 offered promise: large ore chutes with a vein found in no less than a half-dozen places. The Bellevue Mill on the Gold Pan property processed the ore.

By the end of the year, the 30 employees of the Mountain Pride produced 120 tons of ore per month—and anticipated an increase to 200 tons in January.

The Big Snow

The Big Snow and blockade of 1898-1899 brought the mining industry to a standstill. On November 27, 1898, snow began falling. By the next morning, five feet covered Main Street. It snowed every day through February 20, 1898. The Denver, South Park's rotary plows, with much difficulty, kept the tracks to Breckenridge cleared until February 5, 1899. The blockage lasted until April 24, a total of 78 days. Deep snow still fell at higher elevations in July.

Figure 7-5. Rotary Snowplow clearing Snow on the "High Line." When huge bucking plows failed to keep the "High Line" open during the winter of 1898-1899, the railroad brought in its rotary snowplow to tackle the deep snow. (Courtesy Ed and Nancy Bathke)

Despite the blockade, the Mountain Pride during the months of December and January processed 200 tons of milling ore that waited at the Gold Pan mill for shipment. Later, the mill concentrated another 104 tons of ore with a value of $3,909.19.

The 40 men employed on the fifth level, at the end of January, stockpiled ore while sinking a new five-foot by 10-foot shaft.

A New Mill

In mid-April, 1899, the headlines of the *Summit County Journal* announced:

"THE MOUNTAIN PRIDE WILL BUILD A MILL"

The Denver Engineering Works planned a modern, up-to-date 50-ton mill with:
- One Gates crusher, 7x22
- One ore grizzly
- One swinging ore gate
- One automatic feeder
- Two Denver crushing rolls 14x27
- One bucket elevator
- One return screen
- Three sizing screens
- Three Cammett coarse concentrators
- One hydraulic classifying 12 inch
- One hydraulic classifying 20 inch
- Two Cammett concentrators designed expressly for fine concentration
- One mill engine size 15x22 rated 100 HP at 130 revolutions and 80 pounds boiler gauge
- Five Cammett concentrating tables
- Electric light engine size 7x12 rated 18 HP

Chapter 7 Bakers Tank

One 36-inch swinging cut off saw
On electric dynamo 100 lights, 16 candle power
Three horizontal tubular boilers 54x15 feet

Construction began in June. In the middle of July, workers installed the boilers and the 7-ton crusher while carpenters framed the housing for the mill.

Foote built numerous cottages for the employees and a large boardinghouse. An electric motor at the mill furnished light for the mine, mill, cottages, and boardinghouse.

He spared no expense for a Fourth of July celebration at the mine: "At no place in Summit county did patriotism flow more freely on the fourth than at the Mountain Pride mine. The boys up there made up a purse for the occasion and secured a plenteous supply of everything necessary for the approved observance of the day. Friends were invited from Breckenridge, and in the evening the boarding house was transformed into a ball room and the 'light fantastic' was indulged till supper was announced and the guests were seated at a table fairly groaning under its weight of good things prepared under the direction of Mrs. Douglas, who has no peer in the culinary art. Besides dancing, a goodly supply of fireworks had been procured and the participants never missed this portion of a regulation fourth of July celebration. The affair was a grand success in every particular and the Pride boys are to be congratulated."

At the end of July, a correspondent from the *Journal* noted that the Mountain Pride Mining Company, composed of members of the Illinois Steel Company and led by John W. Gates, operated the mine. The new mill, located just west of the new shaft, would be situated so that the ore would be hoisted out of the mine and "practically dumped right into the mill." The company had spent $500 constructing a road to the railroad spur at Bakers tank. A total of 11 buildings, including two bunkhouses, a boardinghouse, and cottages for married employees, cost close to $35,000, a huge sum in 1899.

On August 14, 1899, the *Journal* editor and staff attended a dance and supper in the new mill:

"Although the carpenters are still at work on the building, the boys got together and cleared away the debris in the lower room of the mill, erected a platform for the musicians and arranged a good supply of seats along the walls, making one of the most comfortable and well appointed ball rooms in which the light fantastic toe was ever tripped.

Promptly at 9 o'clock the grand march was announced as a signal for the commencement of the evening's festivities, and the fifteen or more couples present were soon gracefully doing the mystifying figures of this, always, beautiful number. After the grand march, a well selected program was begun and continued with the infatuation and tireless pleasure that is so characteristic of the mountain youth and maiden. At about the midnight hour supper was announced and soon all were seated around a magnificent spread of the most tempting kind it is possible for the hungry appetite to conjure up. This feature of the entertainment furnished by the male portion of the Pride residents and the preparation, arrangement and service of same was left to the more delicate sense of the fitness of things of the ladies, which of itself is a sufficient guaranty that the supper was par excellence, even to the most minute detail; and that the wants of all were looked after with the most careful and painstaking attention. After supper dancing was resumed and continued until after the 'wee sma' hours had departed and the monarch of day began showing his fiery head above the horizon.

Although it rained early in the evening and the weather indications seemed quite unpropitious there were several Breckenridge people present . . ."

By mid-September, the mill had been completed. The telephone company strung lines to the office and depot and extended a long-distance line to the Denver Hotel. Employees had dewatered the shaft next to the mill and driven a drift that connected to the shaft at the old workings. While cutting the drift, the miners encountered an eight-inch streak of lead.

The *Breckenridge Bulletin* on October 6, 1899, screamed:

"It Is the Mountain Pride Mine Near Breckenridge and Is a City in Itself

WILL PRODUCE HEAVILY

With the Best of Management, a Brand New Mill and Backer With Brains, It Grows Greater and Grander With Development . . ."

The article included a history of the mine, production figures, and a description of the mill and mine.

The November 30, 1899, issue of the *Mining Reporter* added even more details. Photographs accompanied the text. R.J.A. Widmer described the new three-compartment shaft, the old shaft, the drift connecting them, and the mill.

Figure 7-6. The Mountain Pride Mill, New Shaft House (to the right), and Tram leading from the Shaft to the Mill. (*Mining Reporter*, November, 1899)

Figure 7-7. Trestle supporting the Ore Tracks carrying Ore from the Shaft House to the Mill, circa 1899. (Courtesy Maureen Nicholls)

Figure 7-8. Crew standing in Front of the Mountain Pride Mill, circa 1899. Note the fire ladders on the roofs and the ore car on the tracks to the right. (Courtesy Maureen Nicholls)

Figure 7-9. Winch for Hoisting the Shaft Elevator at the Mountain Pride, circa 1899. (Courtesy Maureen Nicholls)

Figure 7-10. Mountain Pride Mill in the Winter. (Denver Public Library, Western History Department, X-62411)

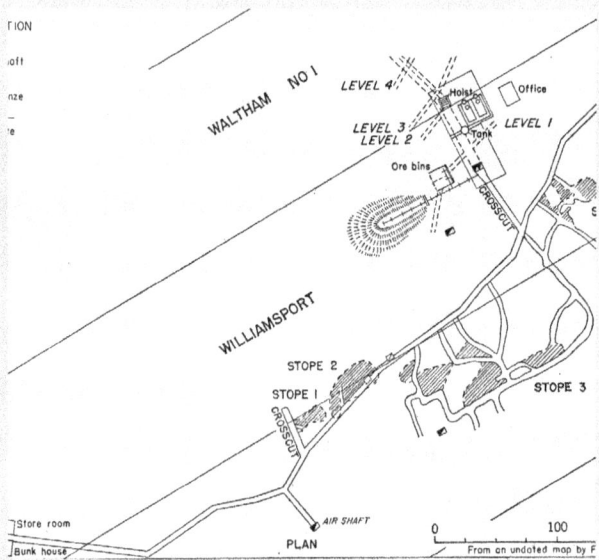

Figure 7-11. Map of the Tunnel System of the Mountain Pride Mine, Birds-Eye-View, circa 1899. (Drawing by F.C. Cramer, included in *Geological Survey Bulletin 970*, 1951)

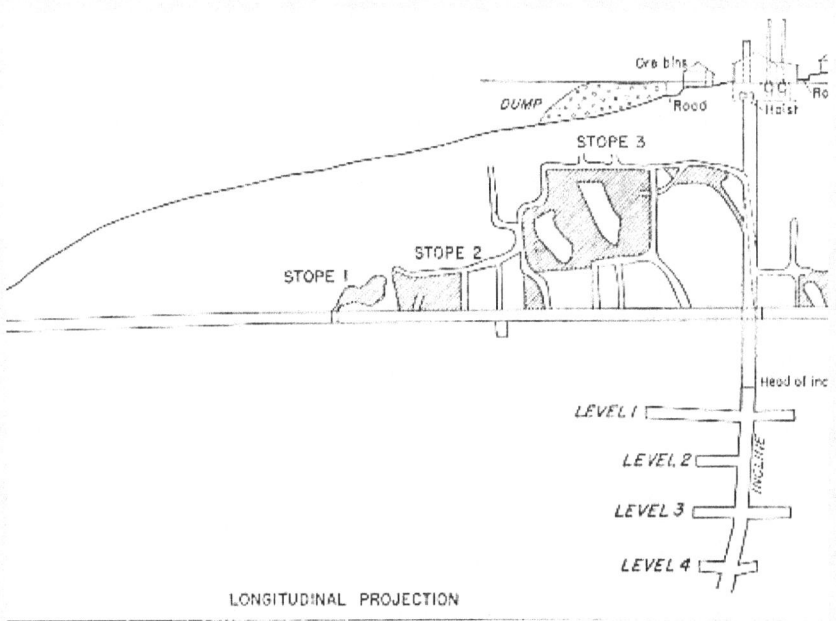

Figure 7-12. Map of the Tunnel System of the Mountain Pride Mine, circa 1899. (Drawing by F.C. Cramer, included in *Geological Survey Bulletin 970*, 1951)

Management Changes and Other News

Throughout 1899 and 1900, the newspapers provided readers with updates on the Mountain Pride mine and mill. In early March, 1900, Henry C. Foote resigned as manager/superintendent to accept a position with a mining syndicate in South America. E.A. LeWald of New York took his place.

Water problems continued in the new shaft.

In May, the *Breckenridge Bulletin* reported that the enrollment at the Mountain Pride school totaled 13 students.

In June, 1900, LeWald resigned and accepted an attractive offer in British Columbia. As a result, work at the mine came to a halt. In July, John W. Gates, president of the Mountain Pride Mining Company, visited Breckenridge with a "view to starting up work again on that property."

New Lessees

However, no news came from the Mountain Pride until November 24, 1900, when the *Summit County Journal* announced new lessees: Robert Foote, C.A. Finding, and Fred Christensen.

By April, miners opened a fine body of ore, greater than anything that had yet been struck on the property. The mill resumed operations. As soon as the snow melted on the road to the railroad spur at Bakers tank, four or five cars of ore and concentrates awaited. When the road opened the first week in July, nine cars carried ore to the Breckenridge sampler [mill].

Forest Fire

By Friday, June 28, 1901, a fire that started on Bald Mountain two days earlier had burned thousands of acres of valuable timber. When

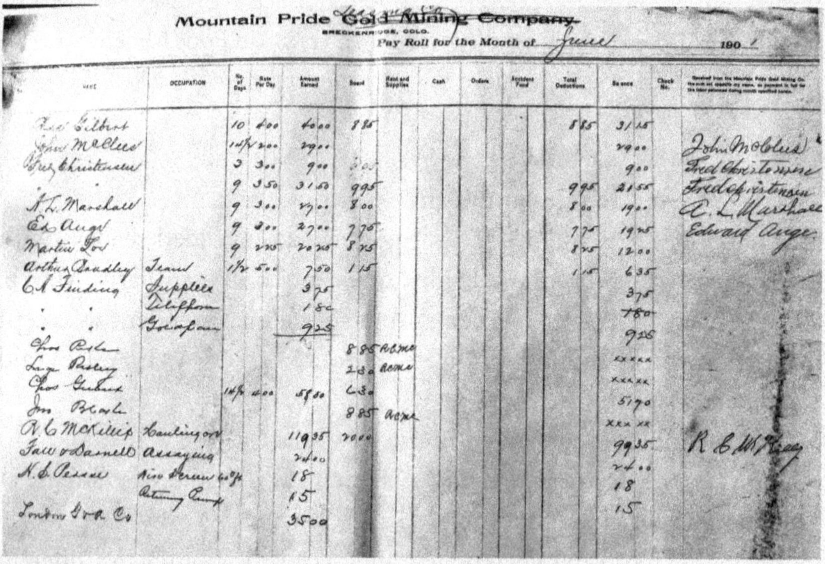

Figure 7-13. Payroll and Expense Log for the Mountain Pride, with Familiar Names such as Ed Auge, C.A. Finding, and R.C. McKillip, 1901. Note the per-day pay of $2 to $5 for a teamster. (Maureen Nicholls)

it reached the Mountain Pride, the fire consumed a dozen cabins and the schoolhouse before totally destroying the mine itself. The huge boilers in the mill provided power to the water pumps that saved the mill from the flames.

New Owners

The newspapers remained silent until January 18, 1902, when the *Summit County Journal* announced that the "Mountain Pride was in New Hands." C.A. Finding, J.K. Bozard, and H.D. Kerr had filed articles of incorporation for the Mountain Pride Gold Mines Company, capitalized at $150,000.

By February they had developed plans to deepen the shaft from its current 250-foot depth after the annual spring water seepage in the shaft evaporated. By the end of March, the mine had been dewatered and the property put into "first-class shape." Once the connections between the old workings had been restored, the owners anticipated operating the mill once again with "no shortage of mill ore."

The mill finally began operating at the end of May, although it operated too slowly. Mr. Shepard from the Denver Engineering Works examined the mill and recommended renovations to improve efficiency.

With the completion of renovations, the Mountain Pride could begin shipping. In July, 1902, two carloads went to the Chamberlain Dillingham sampler [mill] in Breckenridge. In August, three carloads, totaling 159 tons at $40 per ton, had a value of $6,360. Finding reported a net profit for the month of over $2,000.

In September, miners working a new drift in the lower levels of the mine found a five-foot vein of lead ore with high gold and silver values, which the newspaper called "the most important strike ever made in the Breckenridge district." That month, 130 tons of concentrates went to the Breckenridge sampler.

Miners and mine owners proudly displayed specimens from the mines. Often saloons provided exhibit pace for them. Finding showed

Figure 7-14. 600-Pound Piece of Lead-Gold Ore removed from the Mountain Pride Mine in 1902. Robin Theobald, great-grandson of Robert Foote, displays the ore in the entryway of his home in Cucumber Gulch, Breckenridge.

a 600-pound piece of high-grade lead-gold ore from the Mountain Pride at his store in Breckenridge. (*Summit County Journal*, October 25, 1902) It had been a fixture in the Denver Hotel, owned by Robert Foote for many years. Now it sits in the entryway of the Cucumber Gulch home of Robin Theobald, the great-grandson of Foote.

Except for continuing water problems and management turnover, little news came from the Mountain Pride from the end of 1902 until the end of the next year.

Suicide
At the end of May, 1904, news arrived from Tacoma, Washington, announcing that Henry C. Foote, who had been manager/superin-

tendent of the Mountain Pride from May, 1898, until March, 1900, had "killed himself by discharging a gun shot into his ear," leaving a wife and child in New York.

Sheriff's Sale
On September 20, 1904, the *Breckenridge Bulletin* advertised a sheriff's sale of all the mining claims associated with the Mountain Pride, as well as the mill. The sale resulted from a judgment against The Mountain Pride Gold Mines Company and in favor of the Hendrie and Boltholf Manufacturing and Supply Company in the amount of $938.32 plus $5.65 in costs. The newspaper didn't report the outcome of the sale.

Leasing Opportunities
Between December 23, 1905, and March 24, 1906, Charles Finding offered leases on the Mountain Pride: "TO LEASE, to responsible parties the Mountain Pride Mine. Call on C. A. Finding." (*Breckenridge Bulletin*) No one responded.

Delinquent Tax List
As could be expected, in November, 1907, the Mountain Pride properties appeared on the delinquent tax list for 1905-1906.

Historian Rick Hague concluded:
"So, what happened to cause the sudden death of the Mountain Pride, especially considering the glowing reports of rich finds, seemingly good management, and adequate financing? It is impossible, of course, to say. Flooding was undoubtedly an expensive and pervasive problem. Market prices for the mine's main products may have had an influence, but the price of gold was absolutely steady during the mine's life. Silver prices were definitely "in the tank"

during the mine's life, but the mine was not an especially large producer of silver. Management turnover in the latter years of the mine's life certainly did not help. One significant factor – in the author's opinion – is that the mine's ore – while wildly gushed over – probably occurred in relatively small but very rich pockets that were randomly located, isolated, and fairly far apart. Thus, a small pocket of very rich ore might be struck but have a very limited life after expensive development efforts to reach it."

The Mountain Pride Today
The Mountain Pride is one of the most complete and interesting mining properties in Summit County. Part of the mill stands, with its three huge boilers nearly covered with pieces of lumber and other mining debris. The two shaft houses are gone, exposing their collapsed shafts. Numerous log cabins in various stages of disrepair surround the mill. Squatters replaced the roofs on several cabins, preserving them, and built additions to others. The livery stable, deemed the best that Fountain found in the county, had rolling doors at both ends, with hardware still in place. Individual stalls had mangers for hay, stored in the stable's second half-story.

The U.S. Forest Service, the Town of Breckenridge and Summit County share ownership of the property. The town and county closed the road to the mine, allowing only walkers or cyclists to visit. A well-maintained trail from Bakers tank leads to the Mountain Pride. Use the map drawn by Fountain in 2015 (**Figure 7-15**) as a guide to your explorations.

Chapter 7 Bakers Tank

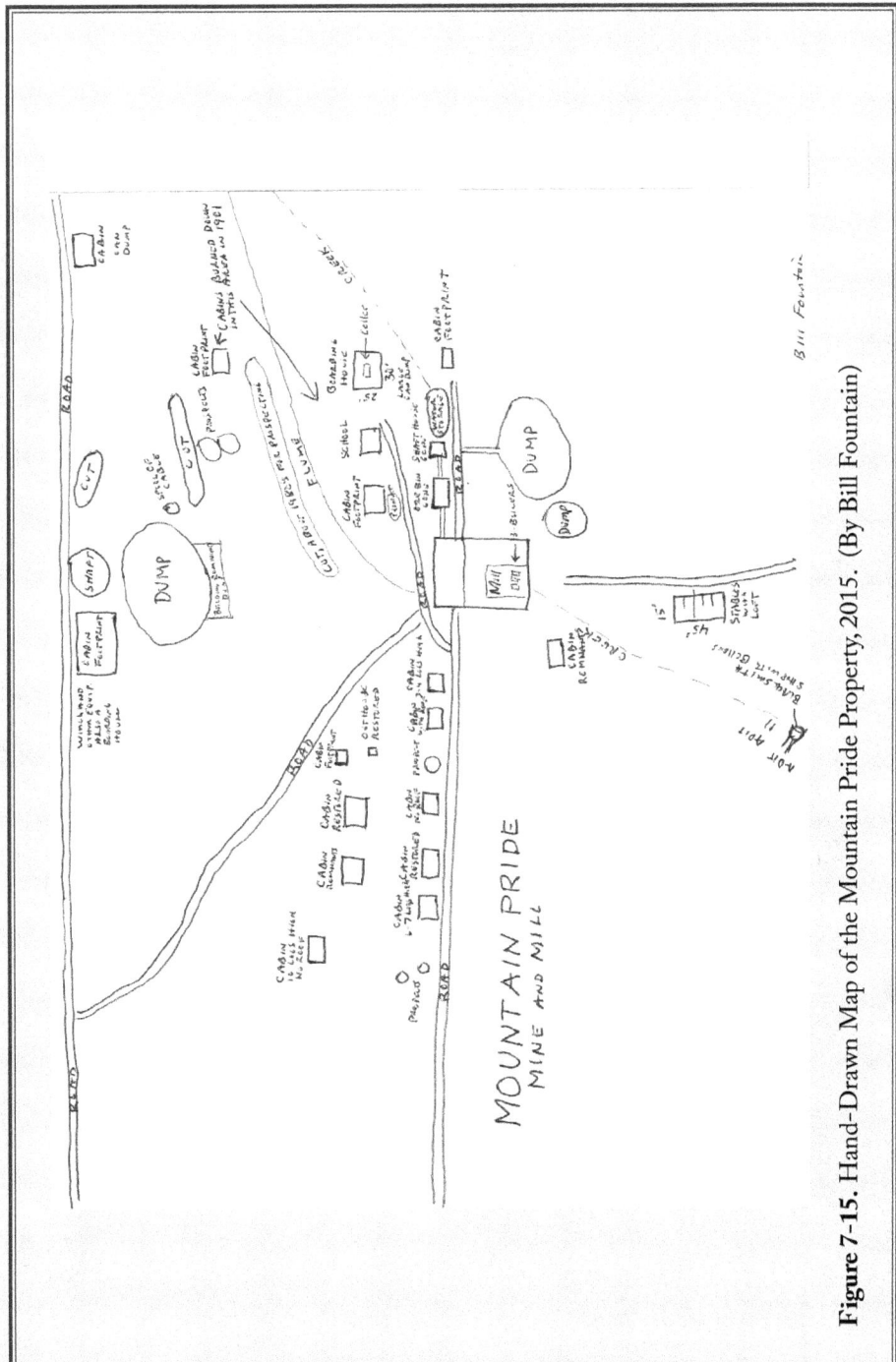

Figure 7-15. Hand-Drawn Map of the Mountain Pride Property, 2015. (By Bill Fountain)

Figure 7-16. The Mountain Pride Mill Skeleton, 1980s. Perhaps the outside boards became "barn wood" for remodeling projects. The skeleton framework clearly shows how the ore moved from the upper to lower levels in a mill. (Courtesy Maureen Nicholls)

Figure 7-17. Collapsed Original Shaft, 2014. Fire destroyed the structure that covered the shaft on March 2, 1898. (Photograph by Author)

Figure 7-18. One of the Restored Cabins, 2014. (Photograph by Author)

Figure 7-19. The Inside of the Cabin seen in Figure 7-18, 2014. The floorboards show evidence of restoration. (Photograph by Author)

Figure 7-20. Remnants in the Foreground, Remodeled Cabin in the Background, 2014. (Photograph by Author)

Figure 7-21. Home Sweet Home—the Inside of the Cabin in Figure 7-20, 2014. (Photograph by Author)

Figure 7-22. Logs and Window Jams from a 115-Year-Old Cabin, 2014. (Photograph by Author)

Figure 7-23. Large Can Dump. Several dumps litter the ground at the Mountain Pride site. (Photograph by Author)

Figure 7-24. Remodeled Cabin with Added Second Story, 2014. A padlock prevented entry. (Photograph by Author)

Figure 7-25. Walls of a Roofless Log Cabin, 2014. (Photograph by Author)

Figure 7-26. Collapsed 15-Stamp Mill, 2014. The mine waste from the newer shaft forms the dumps to the right. (Photograph by Author)

Figure 7-27. Lumber covers Three Huge Rusting Boilers that Generated Steam to operate the Mill, 2014. (Photograph by Author)

Figure 7-28. Mountain Pride Mill, 2014. Rotting lumber and smokestacks from the three boilers cover the hillside. The large tree in the center hides the shaft. (Photograph by Author)

Figure 7-29. Shaft House and Caved-In Shaft, 2014. (Photograph by Author)

Figure 7-30. Dewatering Bucket, 2014. Water presented constant problems in the mine. (Photograph by Author)

Figure 7-31. Large Stable or Barn near the Mill, 2014. The stable had sliding barn doors at both ends, individual stalls with mangers, and a second half-story for holding hay. (Photograph by Author)

Figure 7-32. Manger in the Stable. (Photograph by Author)

Figure 7-33. Collapsed Adit with Evidence of a Blacksmith Shop, 2014. The all-important blacksmith occupied this cabin near the stable and creek. (Photograph by Author)

Figure 7-34. The Blacksmith's Bellows, 2014. (Photograph by Author)

The Mystery of Bakers Tank

Because it proved too small in its original form, the railroad replaced the original water tank (capacity 9,305 gallons) in 1907-1908 with a 10-foot-by-12-foot tank. When this one also proved inadequate, the railroad replaced it with an even larger one measuring 20 feet by 14 feet and holding 47,500 gallons; thus, there existed three Bakers tanks, each one larger than the last. Many historians said the date for the third tank was 1910 with a tank brought from the west portal of the Alpine Tunnel after the company abandoned that line in 1910. Evidence shows that this did not happen.

After conducting extensive research, Kurt Maechner discovered that the tank near the tunnel had, in fact, been moved to Webster, another town along the Colorado & Southern tracks. He published his findings in the January, 2024, issue of *The Bogies & The Loop*, published by the Denver, South Park and Pacific Historical Society. He quotes a 1910 C&S document: "With this I am handing your AFE No. 887 covering an expenditure of $777.25 for renewal of tank at Webster with 14' x 20' tank moved from Alpine Tunnel. You may now proceed with the work." Later company documents verify that this work was completed in February of 1911.

Because lay historians had little easy access to internal C&S documents until Daniel W. Edwards published his series, *The Documentary History of the South Park Line*, incorrect ideas such as Bakers tank being the former Alpine Tunnel water tank had been hard to verify or eliminate.

Thankfully, Edwards' book helped dispel the popular Alpine Tunnel tank myth. So, where did the final incarnation of Bakers Tank come from? Unfortunately, despite his wide-reaching research of C&S records, Edwards found nothing to explain the mystery. On the other hand, the truth may be that the company simply built a larger tank.

The new tank occupied a spot slightly closer to Boreas Pass than the original. The last scheduled passenger train used water from the tank on April 10, 1937; the last freight train took water from the tank the following day. Train crews dismantling the line in the summer of 1938 quite likely used water from the tank but left the tank in place as they moved on.

Chapter 7 Bakers Tank

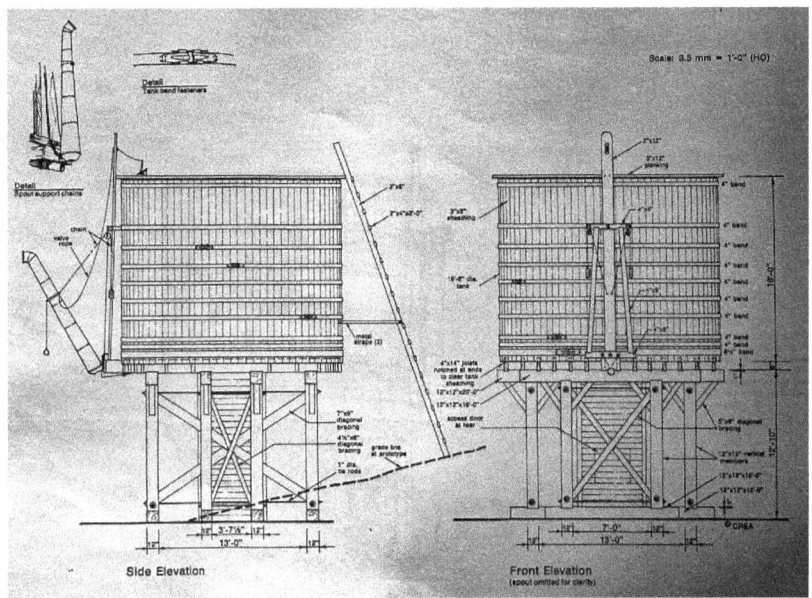

Figure 7-35. Front and Side Elevations of Bakers Tank. (Courtesy Bob Schoppe)

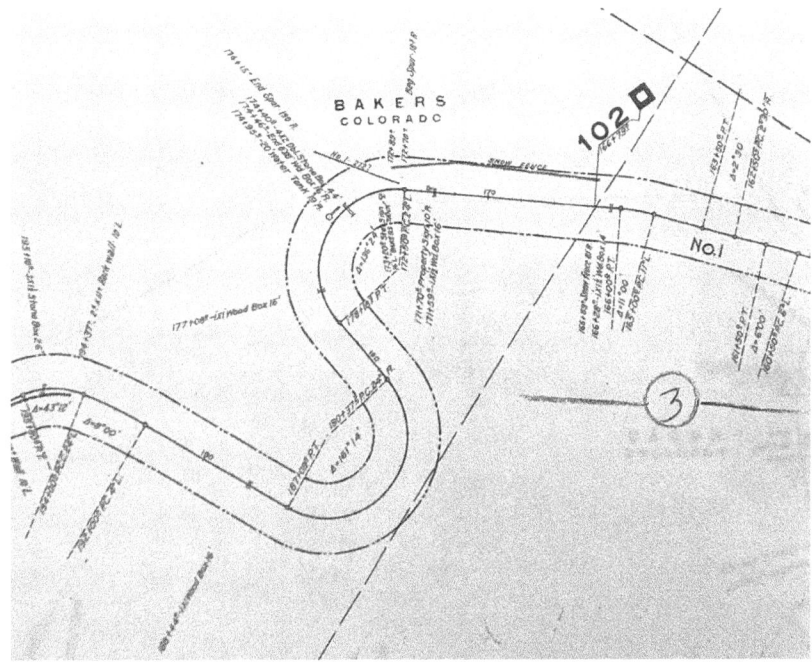

Figure 7-36. Portion of C&S Map with Bakers Tank, 1918. (Courtesy Bob Schoppe)

Figure 7-37. Train with a Rotary Snowplow taking on Water at Bakers Tank, circa 1930. The gentleman on the front, right might have been conductor Roscoe C. Soll. (Denver, South Park & Pacific Historical Society Collection)

Figure 7-38. Eastbound Colorado & Southern Train taking on Water at Bakers Tank, September 12, 1935. (*Denver South Park & Pacific, Memorial Edition*, M.C. Poor)

Restoration

Led by Commissioner Ray F. Hill, the Summit County commissioners restored the tank in 1958.

Figure 7-39. Bakers Tank, September 3, 1950. The ties from the 350-foot spur remain in place. (Denver, South Park & Pacific Historical Society Collection)

Figure 7-40. Bakers Tank, 1950s. (Denver, South Park & Pacific Historical Society Collection)

Figure 7-41. Bakers Tank with the Sign installed by Summit County after the Restoration of the Tank, 1960s. (Courtesy Maureen Nicholls)

Figure 7-42. Bakers Tank, 1970s. (Courtesy Maureen Nicholls)

New Roof for Bakers Tank

In August, 1991, the Summit County Rotary Club installed a new roof on Bakers tank as a service project. (**Figures 7-43, 7-44**)

Figure 7-43. Preparing for a New Roof on Bakers Tank, August, 1991. (Dr. Sandra Mather Collection, Courtesy Breckenridge History)

Figure 7-44. Lowering the New Roof, August, 1991. (Dr. Sandra Mather Collection, Courtesy Breckenridge History)

Twitty's Evaluation

Twitty's site evaluation and map of Bakers tank:
"The tank (F1) is a wood-stave vessel 20' in diameter and approximately 16' high, elevated on a tower standing an additional 12'. A series of ten iron bands with turn-buckles holds the staves together, while a gently pitched plank roof sheds snow in winter. The tower consisted of four piers around the perimeter, holding up 12"x12" stringers, in turn supporting a series of 4"x12" joists. Each pier consisted of two 12"x12" posts tied with 5"x6" diagonal braces. Iron tie rods and 7"x10" diagonal braces join opposite piers together, for additional strength. A plank booth 6'x6' in plan enclosed the tank's 4" drain-pipe within the tower. The tower stands on a foundation of 12"x12" timbers laid across an earthen platform. Graded with cut-and-fill methods, the platform is semicircular and approximately 24' in radius. The tank still features its water nozzle. which pivoted on a small framework of 3"x10" planks. A pier of 4"x6" timbers held the chain and rope for lowering the nozzle, and the timbers had beveled corners for deco-

Chapter 7 Bakers Tank

rative appearance. The tank stands in good condition with crushed gravel paved around the foundation, and an interpretive sign.

A structure stood upslope from and northeast of the tank, and its purpose is uncertain because little evidence is left, but was likely a service building for tools, parts, and possibly an attendant's quarters. Alternately, the structure might have been a rectangular water tank resting on the ground, replaced by the current version in 1910. Currently, a poorly graded platform (F2) approximates the footprint, which was 36'x42' in plan. The platform features two sections. The clearest is a cut-and-fill bench 12'x36' in area outlined with embedded rocks. Extending downslope is a hummocky rectangle of thick grass 30'x36' in plan, with buried rocks outlining the corners. Artifacts are absent, indicating that the structure saw no regular occupation."

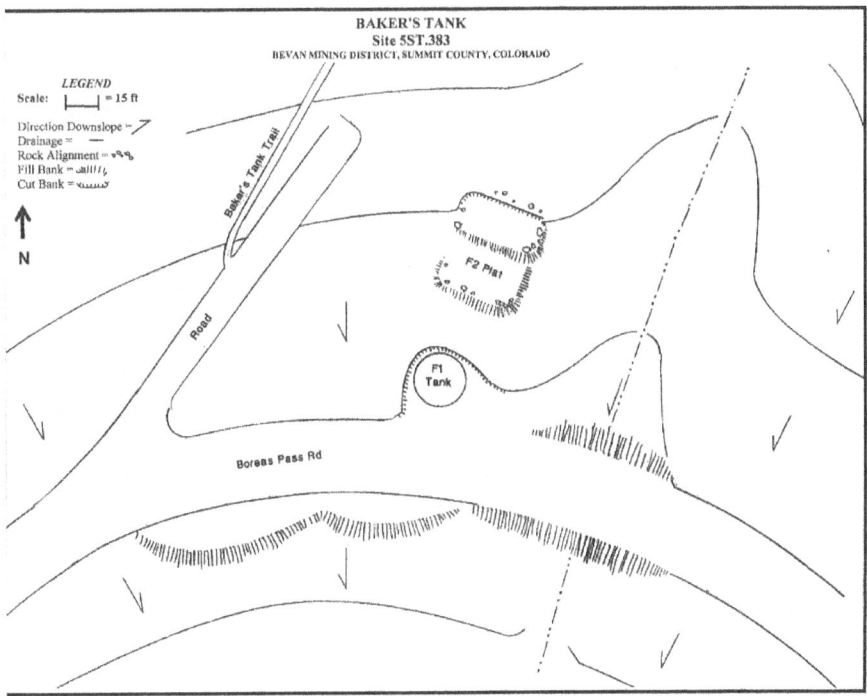

Figure 7-45. Map of Twitty's Bakers Tank Site Evaluation. (Courtesy Mountain States Historical)

Figure 7-46. Bakers Tank, 2021. (Photograph by Author)

Figure 7-47. Aerial View of Bakers Tank. The round, black circle on the middle left indicates the location of Bakers tank. The road on the right coming off the main road approximates the location of the spur. (Google Earth, Imagery ©2021 Maxar Technologies, U.S. Geological Survey, USDA Farm Service Agency, Map data ©2021)

CHAPTER 8
ARGENTINE/BACON STATION

Site Location

At an elevation of 10,604 feet above sea level, Argentine, a station located on the DSP&P High Line at milepost 103.70, 3.7 miles north of Boreas Pass and 6.3 miles south of Breckenridge between Rocky Point and Bakers tank, could not be called a town. The station had a siding that allowed trains coming from opposite directions to pass and provided space to park ore cars awaiting a load of ore from nearby miles. With no commercial buildings, just a station house, ore bin, and platform for loading ore, Argentine existed solely to serve the mines in the area. The railroad changed the name to Bacon in 1906 to honor W.M. Bacon, superintendent of the South Park division of the Colorado & Southern railroad.

Originally, the railroad gave Argentine Station the designation 1136, but by 1902, Colorado & Southern had renamed it Station No. 555.

Figure 8-1. Argentine/Bacon Train Station, 1920. The train on the main line passes cars sitting on the siding. (Denver, South Park & Pacific Historical Society Collection)

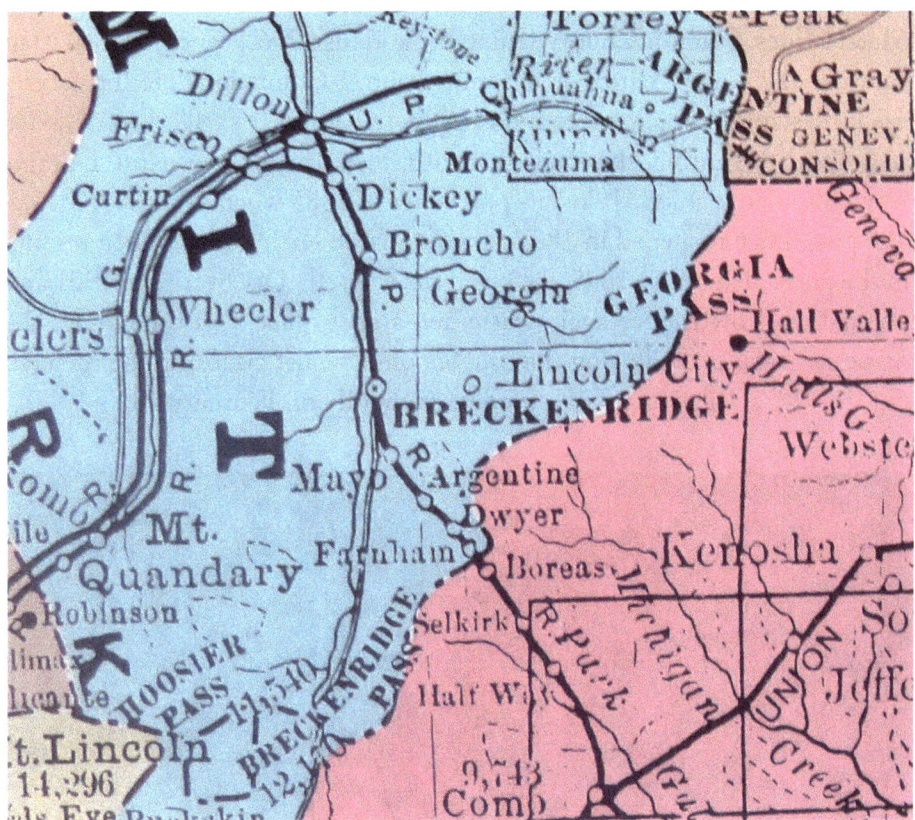

Figure 8-2. Portion of an 1885 Map showing Argentine. (*Crofutt's Grip Sack Guide of Colorado*)

Crofutt's Grip Sack Guide of Colorado in 1885 identified Argentine as a small station on the Breckenridge branch of the Union Pacific railway, five miles from Breckenridge.

Misidentification

Over the decades, many authors confused the railroad station with the town of Argentine, originally named Conger's Camp, located a few hundred yards down the hill to the south.

Even F.C. Cramer, a surveyor in the Breckenridge area, made the error on both his 1900 "Topographical Map of the Blue River Gold Fields and

Metal Mines, Summit County, Colorado" and his 1906 "Topographical Map showing the Metal Mines of Summit County, Colorado." He incorrectly used the symbol for a town to indicate the rail stop.

A third Argentine, this one on Peru Creek, carried the name Decatur when founded in 1868. It lost its post office in 1885 when its mines faltered. The post office reopened in 1891using the name Rathborne. When mining in the area collapsed in 1895, the post office closed. Discoveries in 1901 and population growth once again warranted a post office, this time under the name Argentine. Following the usual boom-to-bust cycle, mining "petered out" in 1907. The post office closed permanently on February 28.

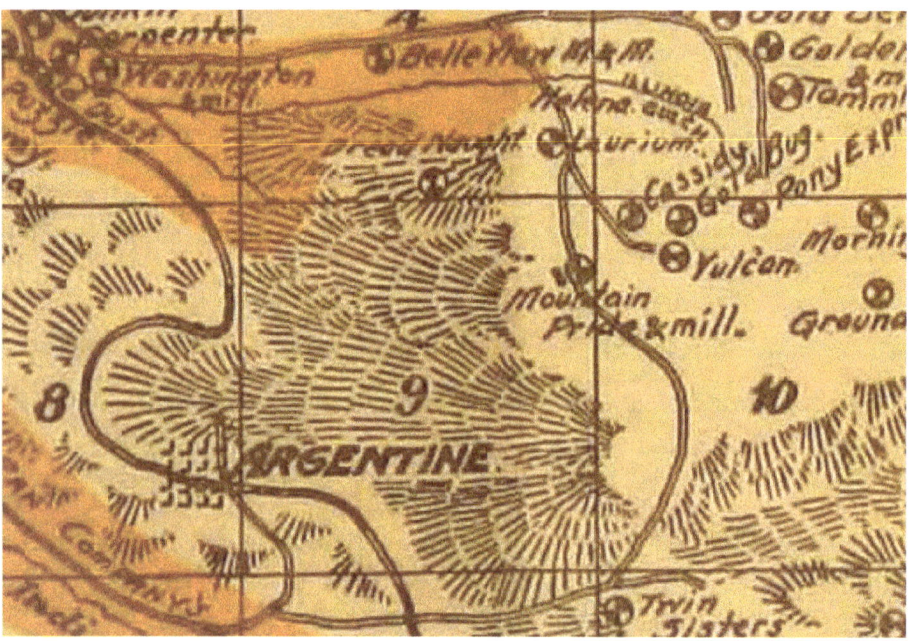

Figure 8-3. F.C. Cramer Map with Argentine Train Station incorrectly identified as a Town, 1900. The Laurium mine, shown on this map, used the Argentine station to ship ore to mills and smelters in Breckenridge, Denver, and beyond. (Author's Collection)

The Laurium Mine and Mill

Eric Twitty completed Colorado Resource Survey Number 5ST.1583 on the Laurium mine in 2019. He identified four distinct areas of development: the main tunnel at the lowest level; the midlevel tunnel; the upper tunnel; and the upper workings. Refer to **Figure 8-18**, the aerial photograph from his report.

Twitty wrote: "Searching the [Illinois] gulch's upper reaches, several miners apparently discovered the Laurium Vein and claimed it during the late 1860s. Over the next ten years, they drove several short tunnels and pecked out small amounts of very rich ore, the era placing the Laurium among Breckenridge's earliest hardrock mines."

The New York & Brooklyn Mining Company purchased the Laurium, previously called the Hoopes mine, for $15,000 in December, 1879. By February, 1880, the company employed 13 men working

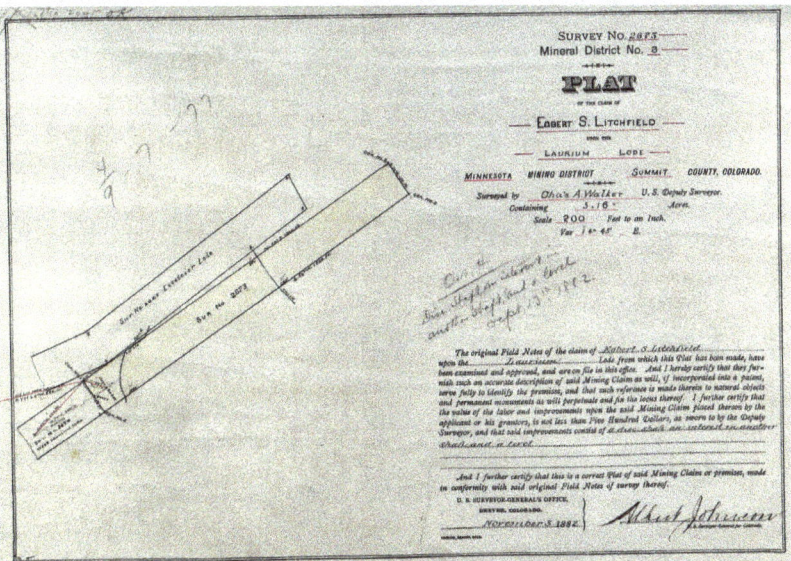

Figure 8-4. Mineral Survey (MS) No. 2673, the Laurium Lode, filed on November 3, 1882. (Courtesy Bureau of Land Management)

under the direction of the company's superintendent, Delos V. Williams. Tunnels at three levels branched off a 60-foot-deep shaft. The assays on the ore showed 173 ounces silver, one ounce gold, and 40 to 60 percent lead.

Twitty continued: "Miners began driving three tunnels roughly 50' apart in elevation on the vein to systematically block it out for extraction. The lower tunnel on the gulch floor was never finished, while the midlevel tunnel higher up the mountainside became the mine's principal point of production."

By September, 1881, the Laurium produced $1,500 per month. The company built a ten-stamp mill at the midlevel tunnel prior to November 3, 1882, when it filed Mineral Survey (MS) No. 2673, Laurium Lode, and Mineral Survey (MS) No. 2674, West Laurium Lode. Note the mill and assay office in **Figure 8-5**.

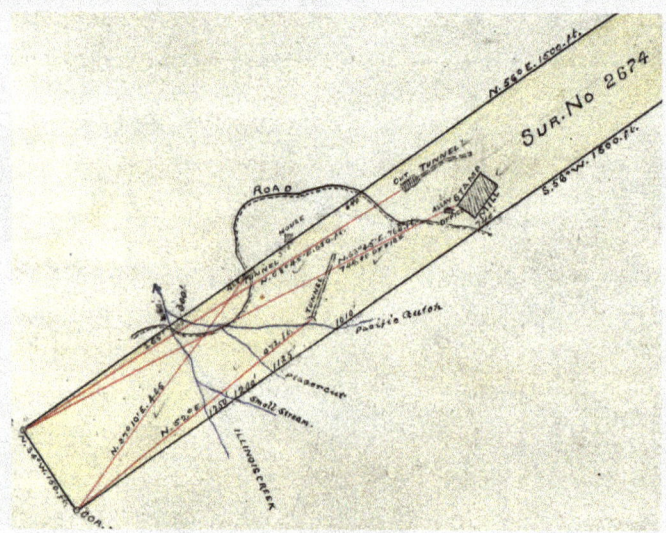

Figure 8-5. Portion of Mineral Survey (MS) No. 2674, the West Laurium Lode, filed on November 3, 1882. The map features identified include the road, house, three separate tunnels, stamp mill, and assay office. (Courtesy Bureau of Land Management)

The *Leadville Weekly Herald* on July 2, 1882, advised that the Laurium mine intended to use the Argentine station to ship its ore.

While newspapers continued their glowing reports of the Laurium through 1887, the mine barely received any notice in 1888 because "The Laurium fifteen stamps [were] in disrepair and idle." Sometime between 1882 and 1888, five more stamps had been added to the mill.

Laurium Mining Company

The *Herald Democrat* (Leadville) followed progress at the mine: "The Laurium is producing some heavy lead ore and will soon ship a car." The Laurium Mining Company, which owned the property, filed a patent application for the Alice E., Laurium No. 2, and Laurium No. 3 on March, 1898, and then leased the property to the Bellevue Mining Company.

Robert Niles and William F. Forman

In June, 1900, according to Twitty: "Robert Niles and William F. Forman [who served as county clerk and recorder at that time] owned the Laurium. With Niles in charge, they decided to develop the abandoned lower tunnel that had been started by the New York & Brooklyn Company in 1880. Niles planned to undercut the main vein at the lowest level possible, exposing a vast tonnage of ore. Late in the year, the tunnel measured 1,100 feet. By driving a lateral drift, the miners encountered the sought-for vein. Even though the vein produced profitable ore, Niles decided to keep lengthening the tunnel. Doing so, he hit the main vein in mid-1902 and could begin steady production."

New Stamp Mill

Niles and financier Forman did not seek outside investors but used the money generated by the mine to continue their operation. In the spring of 1905, they determined that their financial situation would permit constructing a concentration mill to eliminate the high transportation costs incurred when moving their ore to a local concentrator for processing. They would still bear the costs for transporting the concentrates from their mill to a smelter near Denver for final processing.

On October 9, 1905, *The Mining Investor* wrote of the mine's progress and potential:

> "The new five-stamp and concentration mill of the Laurium property in Illinois gulch is running full time on heavy iron sulphide ore from one of the veins which has been opened by the 1,200-foot tunnel. After lots of rough and hard work Messrs. Walker and Niles, who are operating the property, succeeded in opening up a large body of concentrating ore. The vein is said to be from 12 to 20 feet in width. It is probable that an additional battery of five stamps and several more Wilfley concentrating tables will be added to the plant shortly."

Blue Flag Mining & Milling Company

Twitty explained that the mine's potential attracted the attention of investors: "In 1906, the Laurium looked better than ever, and somehow the Blue Flag Mining & Milling Company became aware of the operation. Blue Flag was already a wealthy outfit, running one of the richer gold mines at Cripple Creek, and evaluated the Breckenridge area for undervalued properties. Blue Flag was not alone as investors with other Cripple Creek companies were doing likewise. President J.F. Erisman of Denver negotiated with Niles and bought the Laurium early in 1906, Niles joining the company as a principal. Forman certainly received a good sum for his interest and moved on to run other Breckenridge ventures. From this time onward, the Laurium was known as the Blue Flag Mine."

Chapter 8 Argentine/Bacon Station

Erisman told the *Summit County Journal* on September 29, 1906, that the Colorado & Southern's Argentine station would be renamed Blue Flag because "there were too many Argentines in this state." The Blue Flag company used an ore loading dock on a rail siding at that location. The station did get a new name—but not the one Erisman predicted. The railroad named the station Bacon to honor the superintendent of the South Park Division, W.M. Bacon.

A reporter from the *Breckenridge Bulletin* visited the Blue Flag mine and mill on Monday, December 3, 1906. Five days later, the reporter detailed the extensive development work that had exposed large bodies of milling and shipping ore:

"Ore is removed from the mine through a tunnel, carried on ore cars by gravity to ore bins at the mill near the adit of the mine. The mill was 100 x 26 feet, arranged so the crude ore was carried by its own weight through every point in the concentration process to the place for loading it in the wagon. The mill had a Wallace pulverizer and two Wilfley tables, with room for an additional three. A dynamo had been placed in the mill and electric light was furnished to the mill, mine, houses and blacksmith shop.

Mr. and Mrs. Niles are genial host and hostess, and the party, six in all, were royally entertained."

Although Niles had supervised the mine and mill for six years, Erisman replaced him as superintendent/manager with Charles M. McGrew from Denver in January, 1907.

A New Power Source

A new power source—electricity—arrived in the county at the turn of the century. Its use slowly spread across the mining landscape. In June

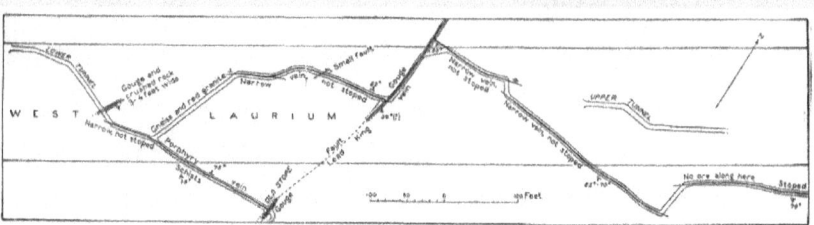

Figure 8-6. Map with the Lower Tunnel and Portion of the Upper Tunnel of the Laurium Mine, 1909. Note the names of the rocks intersected by the tunnels: granite and porphyry, both igneous; gneiss and schist, both metamorphic. (F.R. Ransome, *USGS Professional Paper, No. 75*)

and July of 1908, Blue Flag closed their mill to begin its conversion to electric power. All of those working in the mill lost their jobs while the company replaced most of the machinery. Unfortunately, just as the company finished the renovations, legal problems prevented the Summit County Power Company from extending its power line from Dillon to the mine. Nevertheless, the power line eventually reached the newly renovated mill at an unknown later date.

When Ransome visited Summit County conducting research for his *USGS Professional Paper No. 75*, he found only the Laurium and three other mines (the Wellington, Country Boy, and Sallie Barber) producing and shipping ore. He noted that the value of the pyritic concentrate with some gold and silver produced by the Laurium's 60-ton mill totaled $80,000 but he did not indicate the time period involved. Refer to **Figure 8-6** for a map of the "principal level of the Laurium mine."

Excerpt for a legal notice in November, 1911, listing the Laurium and West Laurium lodes on the Summit County delinquent tax list, little appears about either lode until.........

Back in Business

The headline in the *Summit County Journal & Breckenridge Bulletin* on November 4, 1911, shouted: "**BLUE FLAG DEVELOPING**, the mill and other buildings have all been painted, several 'caves' in the tunnel have been caught up and things are in good shape for the winter campaign. As soon as the transformers arrive and are placed in position, a cross-cut will be started and the machine drill set to work. Joe Marz of Breckenridge is in charge and states that only development work will be done during the winter."

The year 1912 brought two interesting events: On June 24, President Erisman, accompanied by his wife and the Board of Directors of the Blue Flag Mining & Milling Company, arrived in a special railroad car at the Bacon spur. The group toured the Laurium mine and mill. In August, a Colorado & Southern train brought several officers and stockholders of the Blue Flag Company for a similar tour.

The company faced problems, as Twitty explained: "The Laurium . . . increased production in 1912, and the company had to refit the mill's crushing sequence again in 1913. A new jaw crusher and grinding appliance known as a crushing rolls replaced the Wallace machines, which were worn out and probably obsolete. But even with better crushing, the mill was no longer recovering as much of the ore's metal content as it should have, suggesting that the vein further changed in character with even greater depth. The investors grew unhappy with the prospect of refitting the mill once more, so they suspended further operations in 1914 and studied the problem. An easy solution never arrived, however, and rebuilding the mill seemed to be the only option, raising doubts about whether the huge expense would be repaid.

Despite the troubles, the mine and mill produced through 1917 and into 1918 under the direction of Joe Marz until B.F. Hall replaced him as superintendent in November, 1918. Production continued intermittently through 1920 when the company installed a new ball mill. Shortly thereafter, an economic recession gripped the country. The investors chose not to continue financing the mine and mill."

Historian Maureen Nicholls shared photographs of the Laurium mine and mill complex from the 1920s and 1930s. (**Figures 8-7** through **8-13**)

Figure 8-7. The Laurium Mine and Mill Complex, 1920s. The tall mill stands behind the assay office. (Courtesy Maureen Nicholls)

Figure 8-8. Portal of the Laurium Gold Tunnel. Second from left, James Galloway, mining engineer; center, L.E. Webster, manager. (Courtesy Maureen Nicholls)

Figure 8-9. The 1905 Mill at the Laurium, 1920s. (Courtesy Maureen Nicholls)

Figure 8-10. The 1905 Laurium Mill to the Left; Mine Buildings to the Right, 1920s. (Courtesy Maureen Nicholls)

Figure 8-11. Boardinghouse at the Lower Tunnel of the Laurium Complex, 1920s. The ladders on the roof could be used to help fight a chimney fire. (Courtesy Maureen Nicholls)

Figure 8-12. Log Cabins at the Laurium Mine and Mill, 1920s. Logs form the walls of the cabin on the left while hewn logs form the walls of the main cabin on the right. (Courtesy Maureen Nicholls)

Figure 8-13. Winter at the Laurium Mine. (Courtesy Maureen Nicholls)

The 1930s, 1940s, and 1950s

Colorado mine reports and the *Mineral Yearbook* provide information from these decades.

In 1934, the Laurium Gold Consolidated Company with James D. Galloway, manager, and Vern C. Howard, superintendent, owned the Laurium where employees cleared a cave-in from a 2,000-foot-long tunnel. A log cabin near the tunnel housed a blacksmith shop and changing room.

George Robinson owned the Blue Flag in 1935. Operators (lessees of the property) included G. E. Twiby, W. Greg, and A.M. Gabrial, who mined the 1,400-foot-long midlevel tunnel and shipped ore by train to Leadville smelters using the Dunkin switch. In the lower tunnel, the state mine inspector observed a cave-in and, on the valley floor, some buildings at the Laurium tunnel. Robinson served as Summit County treasurer from 1907 until 1940.

The *1937 Mineral Yearbook* attributed minor production to the Laurium, with ore being shipped to Leadville smelters. In 1939, the same publication credited the Blue Flag with shipping a small tonnage of ore, again, to Leadville. Although the *1940 Mineral Yearbook* noted minor production, the *Summit County Journal* announced some hopeful news on November 22, 1940: "Good progress is being made on the new tunnel at the Blue Flag." The 1948 yearbook repeated its previous entry: minor production.

Finally, in 1957, the Colorado mine report included the last information about the Laurium /Blue Flag mine: Frank Brown, owner, and Mayard F. Ayler, Carl Keaettly, and Martin Legere, lessees. Frank Brown, Summit County treasurer from 1940 to 1974 and the mayor of Breckenridge from 1946 to 1964, and his wife, Theta, told many interesting tales about mining in Summit County and the history of Breckenridge during those decades.

Hippies at the Laurium

In the 1970s, hippies, coming to the Breckenridge area seeking a more free-spirited lifestyle, renovated some of the buildings remaining from mining days. Needing a place to live summer and winter, they repaired walls and roofs. According to Robin and Patty Theobald, several young people, who called themselves freaks, fixed up two or three of the still-standing cabins at the Laurium's lower tunnel in 1969 and lived rent-free for three or four years. Theobald recalled vising some friends there.

Figure 8-14. The Lower Tunnel of the Laurium Mine and 1905 Mill, 1960s. (Courtesy Maureen Nicholls)

The 1970s and 1980s

During these decades, Barney Brewer, a local real estate broker, owned a portion of the 104-acre Laurium site. When the group sold the property, Barney retained a 10 percent interest.

Brewer, an avid cross-country skier, operated The Breckenridge Ski School Experience on the property from about 1976 until 1990. He rebuilt the log cabin, chinked between the logs with cement, installed a new roof, and added an old wood stove. A small cabin next to the renovated cabin near the collapsed adit of the lower tunnel became the sauna. Water draining from the tunnel he heated to provide steam for the sauna. He also moved the outhouse to the hillside, away from the log cabin, where it still sits today.

Brewer's son, Ben, told of the experience enjoyed by the guests:
> "His school operated as a day program, with basic skills taught in the morning on the Laurium mine property. Then, folks would be treated to a gourmet lunch of homemade soup and sandwiches made by his ex-wife, Kate Brewer, also an avid cross-country skier.
>
> In the afternoon, the guests would be treated to a true back country adventure using their newly acquired cross country ski touring skills. Barney would lead them from the Laurium property, through to Boreas Pass Road at the meadow and down to the winter gate and trail head where they would be met by a van. Along the way he taught them lessons on avalanche safety, how to build a survival snow cave, hypothermia, advanced ski touring techniques and many of his tips and tricks for getting around in the winter in the back country. People simply loved these lessons and the experiences they had as a part of this unique ski school. Whole families and larger groups from all over the country

and other parts of the world took part … and at the end of the trail, participants received a small pin as a keepsake of their experience."

Figure 8-15. Barney Brewer and a Breckenridge Ski Touring Experience Sign. (Courtesy Ben Brewer)

Figure 8-16. Buildings at the Lower Tunnel of the Laurium Mine, 2003. In the 1970s, hippies, coming to the Breckenridge area seeking a more free-spirited lifestyle, renovated some of the buildings. Seeking a place to live summer and winter, they repaired walls and roofs. More than likely, they renovated some of the buildings they found at the Laurium. Had it not been for them, these buildings might have collapsed long ago. (Photograph by Author)

Figure 8-17. The 1905 Laurium Mill, 2003. (Photograph by Author)

Chapter 8 Argentine/Bacon Station

New Owners for the Laurium

In 2014, the Town of Breckenridge Open Space & Trails and Summit County Open Space & Trails purchased the 104-acre Laurium property for $850,000 anticipating limited non-motorized winter and summer recreational purposes.

Twitty Photographs

Figures 8-18 through **8-29** come from Eric Twitty's Colorado Resource Survey of the Laurium, number 5ST.1583. The numbers in parentheses refer to items on the map.

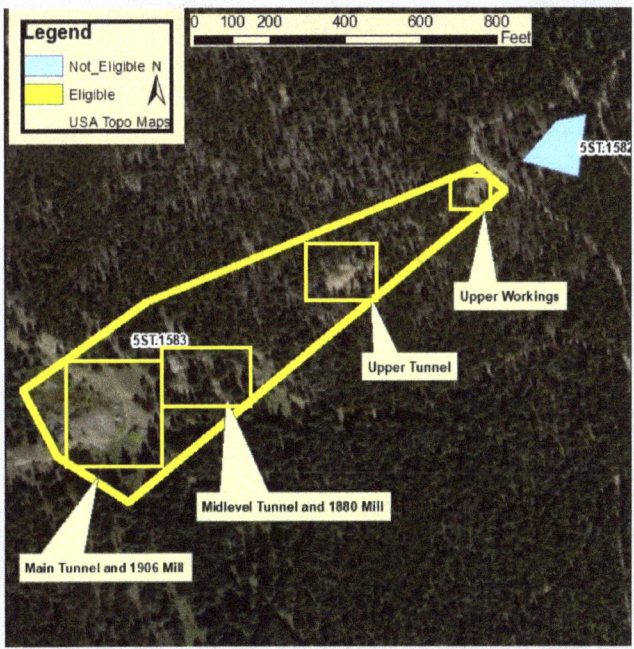

Figure 8-18. Aerial View of the Laurium Mine Complex showing the Main Tunnel and 1905 Mill, the Midlevel Tunnel and 1880 Mill, the Upper Tunnel, and the Upper Workings. (Courtesy Mountain States Historical, Eric Twitty)

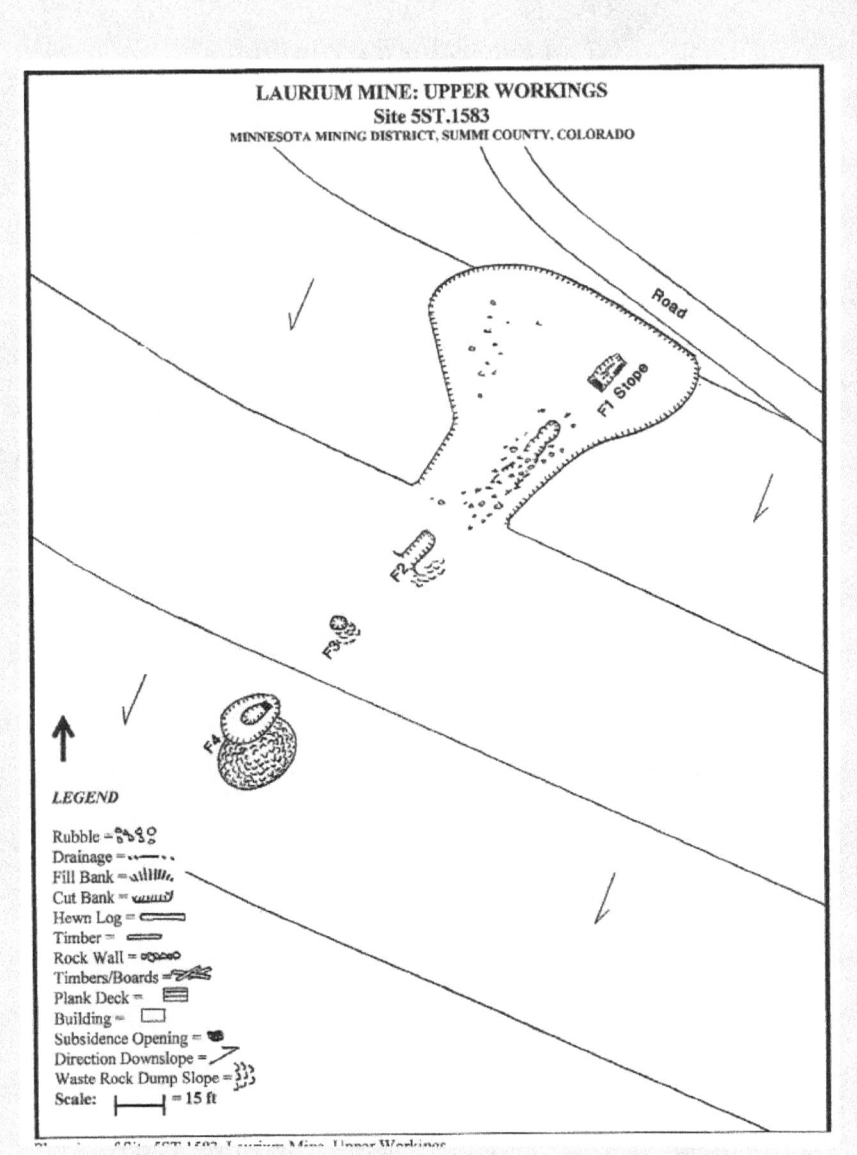

Figure 8-19. Site Map of the Upper Workings of the Laurium Mine Complex. (Courtesy Mountain States Historical, Eric Twitty)

Figure 8-20. Prospect Shaft in the Upper Workings (F4), 2021. (Courtesy Mountain States Historical, Eric Twitty)

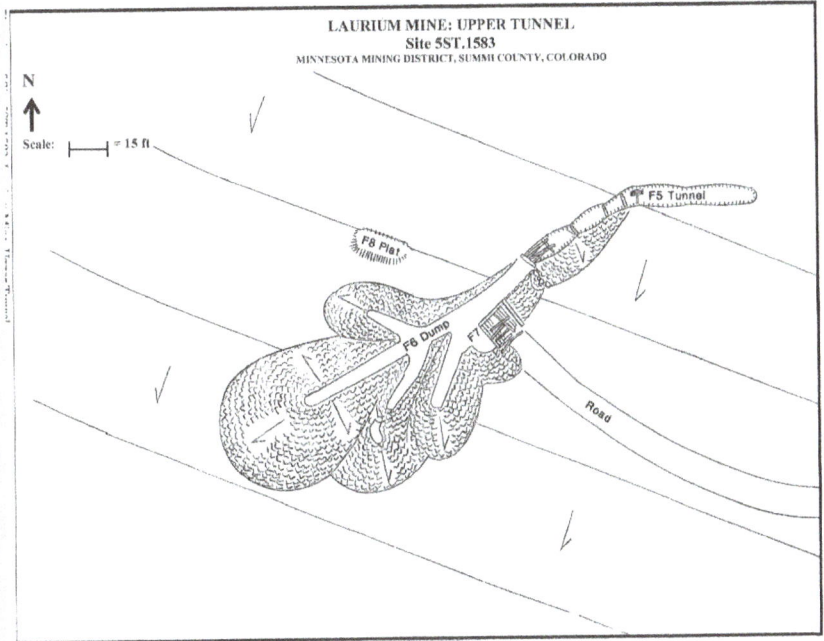

Figure 8-21. Site Map of the Upper Tunnel of the Laurium Mine Complex. (Courtesy Mountain States Historical, Eric Twitty)

Figure 8-22. Upper Tunnel (F5), 2021. (Courtesy Mountain States Historical, Eric Twitty)

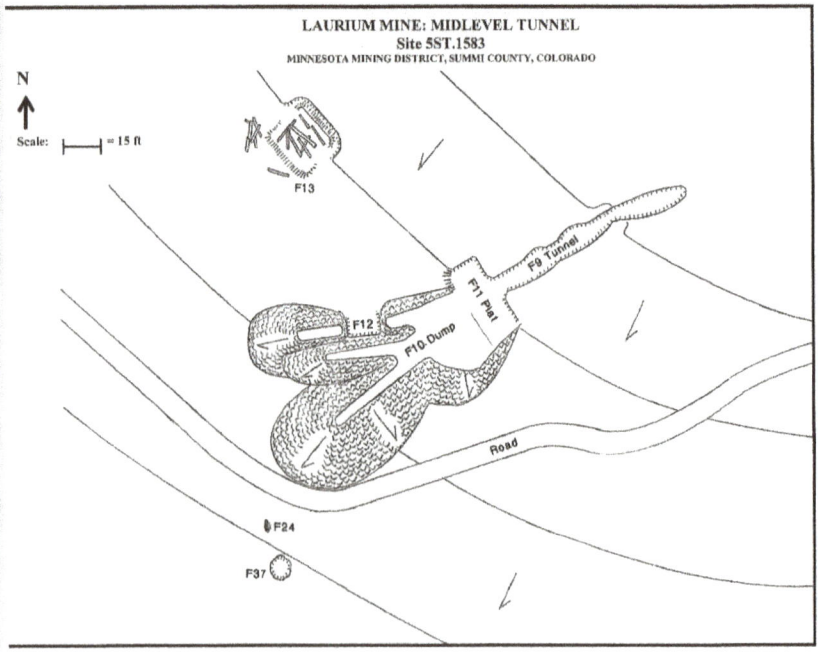

Figure 8-23. Site Map of the Midlevel Tunnel of the Laurium Mine Complex. (Courtesy Mountain States Historical, Eric Twitty)

Figure 8-24. Remains of the Boardinghouse at the Midlevel Tunnel (F13), 2021. (Courtesy Mountain States Historical, Eric Twitty)

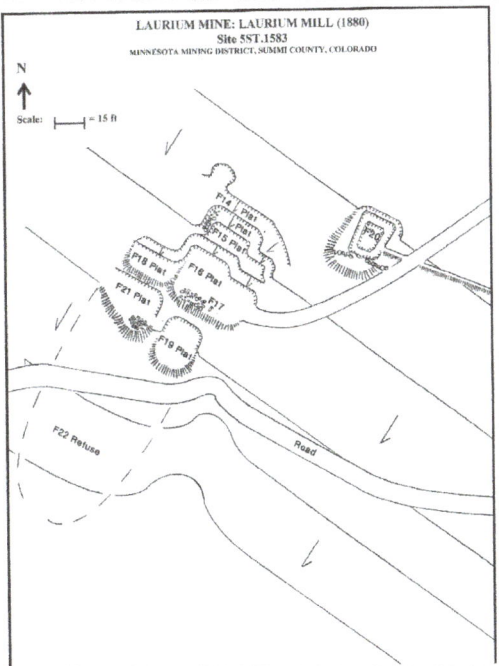

Figure 8-25. Site Map of the 1880 Mill of the Laurium Mine Complex. (Courtesy Mountain States Historical, Eric Twitty)

Figure 8-26. Location of the 1880 Mill (F14-F16), 2021. (Courtesy Mountain States Historical, Eric Twitty)

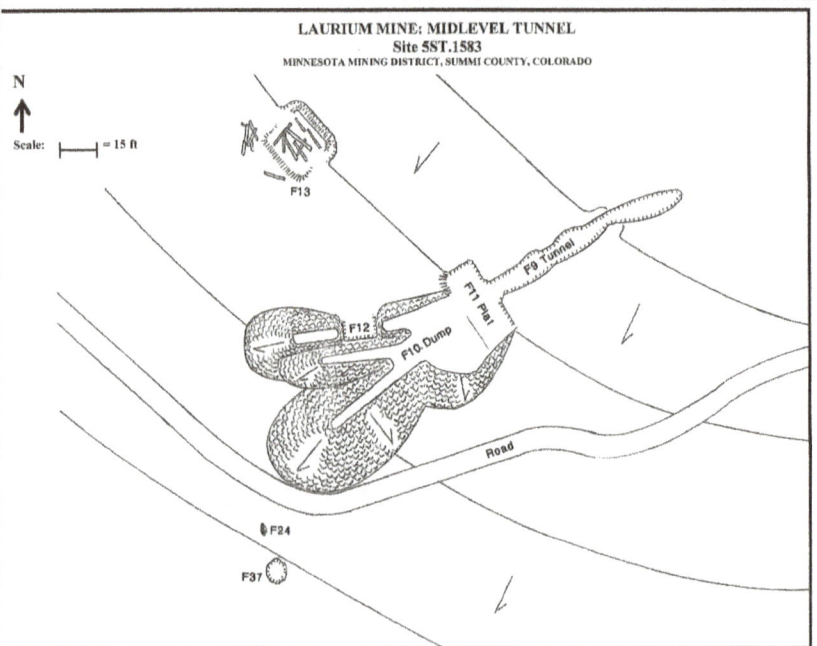

Figure 8-27. Site Map of the Lower Tunnel and 1905 Mill of the Laurium Mine Complex. (Courtesy Mountain States Historical, Eric Twitty)

Chapter 8 Argentine/Bacon Station

Figure 8-28. Lower Level of the Laurium Mine Complex, 2019. The lower tunnel (F23), just off this image in the lower right, has collapsed. The white building (F25) holds the equipment added in recent decades to treat the water draining from the mine. The log cabin, expertly rehabilitated in 1982, held the blacksmith shop (F27). The boardinghouse (F30) sits to the upper left. (Courtesy Mountain States Historical, Eric Twitty)

Figure 8-29. Remains of the 1905 Mill at the Lower Level of the Laurium Mine, 2019. (Courtesy Mountain States Historical, Eric Twitty)

Figure 8-30. Panoramic View of the Laurium. The lower workings are on the left and the mill ruins are on the right. (Photograph by Author)

Figure 8-31. Aerial View of the Laurium Mine Lower Level and 1905 Mill Site, 2021. The remnants of the mill can be seen in the middle of the image. A few buildings that remain appear on the right. (Google Earth, Imagery ©2021 Maxar Technologies, U.S. Geological Survey, USDA Farm Service Agency, Map data ©2021)

Little exists in writing about Argentine station. The map in **Figure 8-32** shows the site in the early 1900s. One of numerous Summit County train wrecks occurred at the station in 1900. (**Figure 8-33**)

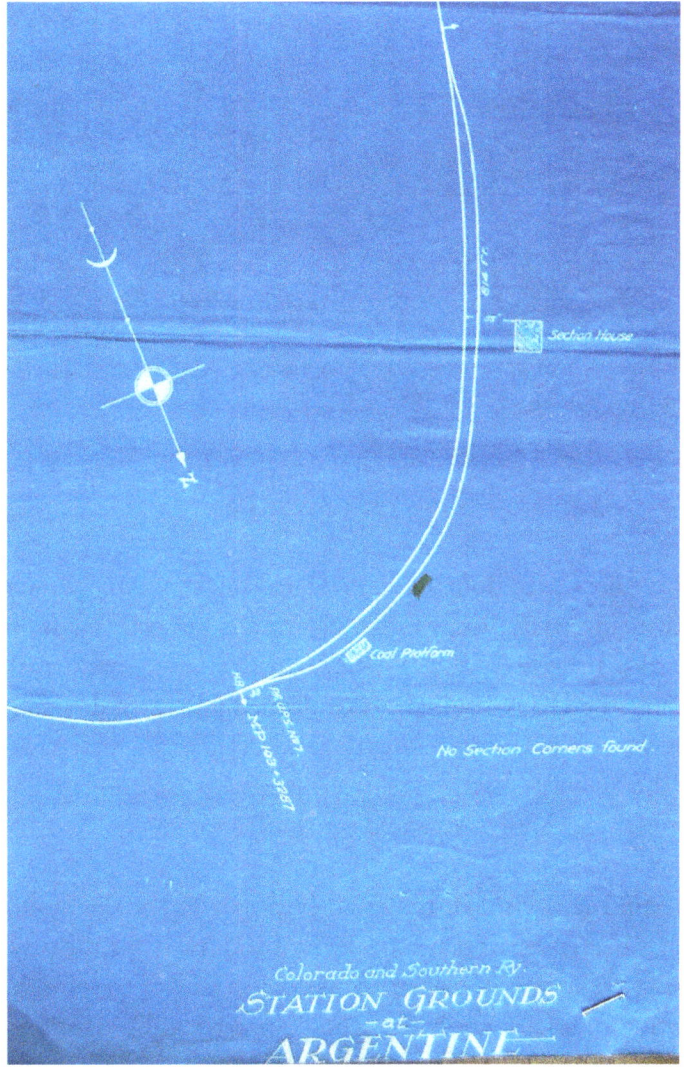

Figure 8-32. Map showing the Argentine Station, circa 1900. By this time, the Colorado & Southern had assumed ownership from the bankrupt Denver, Leadville & Gunnison. The railroad siding can be seen to the right of the main track. (Denver, South Park & Pacific Historical Society Collection)

Figure 8-33. Train Wreck at or near Argentine, circa 1900. (Denver, South Park & Pacific Historical Society Collection)

Snow on Boreas Pass

When heavy snow over Boreas Pass hindered rail service between Como and Breckenridge, citizens of Breckenridge felt that the company made little effort to clear the tracks. In early April, 1911, the railroad reported that snow blocked the tracks. Although a Denver newspaper confirmed that the railroad sent crews to clear the tracks west of Como, serious doubts existed on the part of Breckenridge residents. The *Summit County Journal & Breckenridge Bulletin* hired Sam Blair to learn the truth. The April 8 issue told the story in great detail:

> "Mr. Sam Blair, who has traversed every portion of the mountains, who has been over Boreas Pass, by trail and track, for the past forty years, and who would have no other object except to state the true condition of affairs, took a notebook along and brought back the following report:
>
> 'At Bacon, for one-quarter of a mile, there is an average of two feet of snow; there is absolutely no ice on the tracks. Between Bacon and Bakers tank there are only two drifts, one being about 150 feet

in length and six feet deep; another 50 feet long, averaging four feet on one rail, the other rail being clear; with small drifts here and there. Between Bakers tank and Dyer there is one big drift 300 feet long, in which the snow-plow would have to be used. From Dyer to Farnum the greater part of both rails is clear. From the turn above Farnum snow averages two feet nearby to the top of Boreas, from which point the track is absolutely clear until the first shed entrance is reached.

In No. 1 shed, at Boreas, for 100 feet there is no snow. About the center of the shed, at the mail hole opening, which was carelessly left open, allowing the north wind to blow in, there is an average of three feet of snow, no ice.

No. 2 shed has a similar mail hole, with a northern exposure, but in that shed there is only one drift ten feet long averaging about six feet deep; 200 feet from east entrance track is clear.

No. 3 is a short shed, open clear through.

No. 4 shed is the worst of all. This shed has two holes in the north side, and for about 200 feet in the center there is a drift which would have to be shoveled out and hauled out on flat cars. The snow stands high—within three feet of the roof—but Mr. Blair and his faithful dog went through, nevertheless.
There is no ice on the tracks in any of the sheds, the water from the roofs falling on the snow and freezing before it reaches the rails.

Nos. 5 and 6 sheds are practically clear of snow, and there is no ice on the rails whatever.

Between Nos. 2 and 3 sheds there is about 700 feet of snow, averaging 15 feet in depth, which would have to be taken off with a rotary [snowplow]. Messrs. Bacon and Melin walked over the top of it. Mr. Melin had rigged up a pair of impromptu snowshoes

[skis] from a couple of boards which he found at a cabin, but abandoned them after a short time.

A few miles above Breckenridge all trace of shovel and pick work disappeared, and as for snowplows—why, the signs of their prolonged and entire absence were simply overwhelming.'

The above is an accurate statement of traffic difficulties over Boreas, and while it is not our object to tell the railroad company how to manage its line, we feel it our duty to expose the falsehoods published in Denver, the source of which stories is only too obvious. If the South Park branch of the Colorado & Southern had really wanted to open its line from Leadville to Como on or about the first of April, as Senator John S. Cary, through a phone conversation with this paper, informed the people of Summit County would be the case, the road could have been cleared for traffic with a force of 20 men and the rotary in ten hours. It looks now as if we will have to take our medicine and look pleasant, as Mr. Cary is not enough interested in his constituency hereabouts even to attempt an explanation. The *Journal-Bulletin* goes into practically every home in Summit County, beside reaching to every other state in the Union and over the wide sea and we pledge our columns to give the lie to hired news articles when the real facts are to be had; and it is our belief that these falsehoods have been published with the intention of retarding the re-establishment of the Breckenridge-Como service to the last possible moment."

The newspaper followed the on-going efforts to force the railroad to meet its obligations:
"Division Superintendent John Dwyer and Roadmaster A. Malin, of the Colorado & Southern railway, came up from Denver on Wednesday. The train took them up the hill a short distance beyond the Bacon siding, and from there they walked over Boreas pass to Como, meeting other officials on the way who had climbed the eastern slope. It is said the trip was made to inspect the roadway in

order to ascertain just how much work is needed to place the road in proper condition to run trains between Breckenridge and Como." (*Summit County Journal & Breckenridge Bulletin*, April 9, 1912)

Heavy Snow

A huge snowstorm at the end of February and into the first week of March, 1913, stopped all trains from Denver. With the snow too deep for huge bucking plows, the railroad brought in the rotary snowplow and had the track cleared by 11:30 p.m., Friday, March 6. The rotary was followed "by three engines and caboose backing down from Bacon siding, a train made up of an engine, a combination coach and Superintendent Conroy's car, they being followed by the regular passenger train from Denver, they met the east-bound passenger here, which then proceeded on to Denver."

The article added: "The rotary started out of Como yesterday morning at 7 o'clock, bringing about 15 snow shovelers, eight or ten passengers and express matter. Trouble was encountered about two miles east of Boreas and the rotary was kept constantly in motion from there into the yards at Breckenridge. Frequent stops were enforced while the ice had to be dug out from the track by the use of the pick. More trouble was encountered on this piece of road yesterday perhaps than has been experience in some years."

Breckenridge from Rocky Point

In her book, *Colorado Pioneers in Picture and Story*, published in 1915, Alice Polk Hill describes her train trip from Como to Breckenridge. She wrote:

"At Rocky Point, where we reach the acme of scenic glory on this line, the town of Breckenridge commences to play 'Bo-peep' with the admiring tourist; first on this side and then on that, we see it—making another turn, a full view is obtained.

The pretty little frontier town seems only a stone's throw distance, but the train, as if in a frolicsome mood, with no other aim than to intensify our interest in the play, dashes away, making a short curve and surprises the town from another point."

Figure 8-34. Rotary Snowplow clearing Snow. Men hired by the railroad cleared the tracks of any remaining ice and snow after the rotary passed. Should a drift be too deep for the rotary, the men shoveled the top of the drift down to the level of the rotary. (Courtesy Maureen Nicholls)

Figure 8-35. Shovelers clearing the Track. The snow to the right measured more than 12 feet deep; that on the right about eight feet deep. (Courtesy Maureen Nicholls)

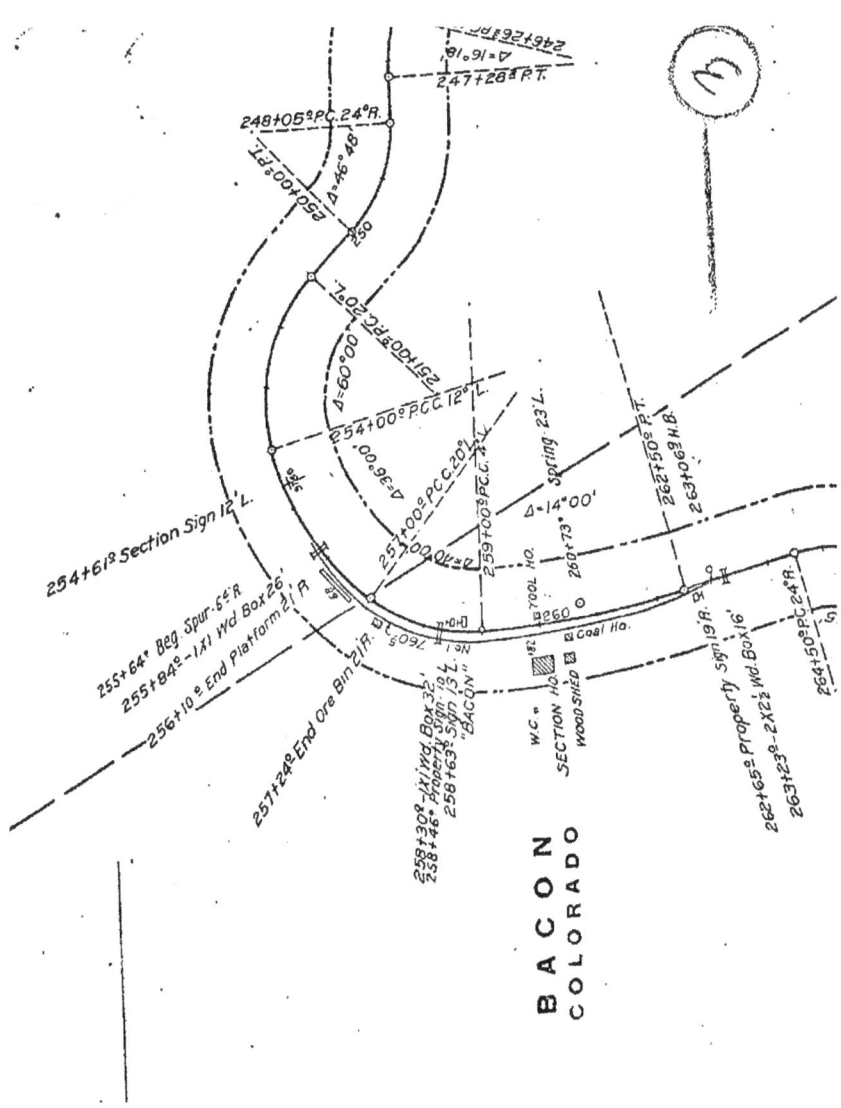

Figure 8-36. A 1918 Map showing Bacon Station, Section House, Woodshed, and Coal Bin paralleling the Siding. A sign along the siding announced "Bacon." (Denver, South Park & Pacific Historical Society Collection)

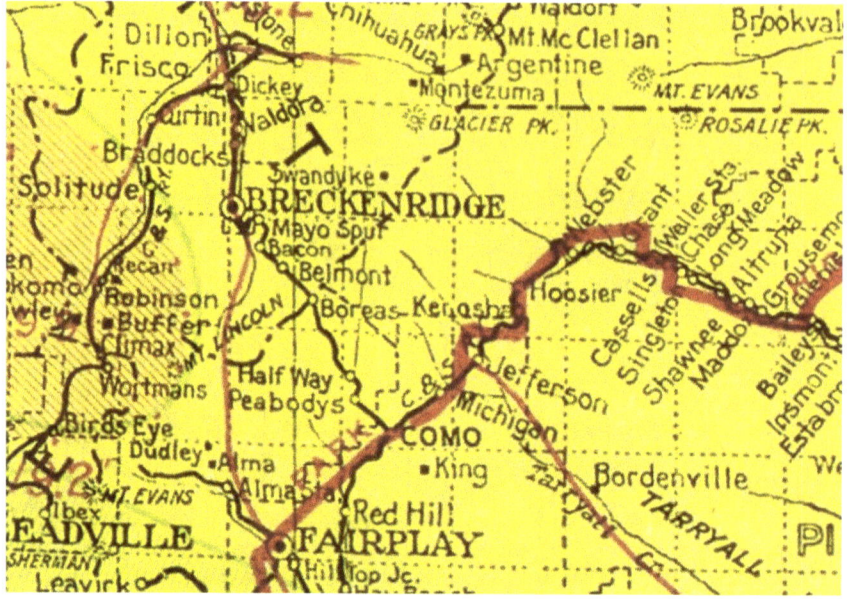

Figure 8-37. Portion of a 1918 Colorado Map showing Bacon and Belmont. (Author's Collection)

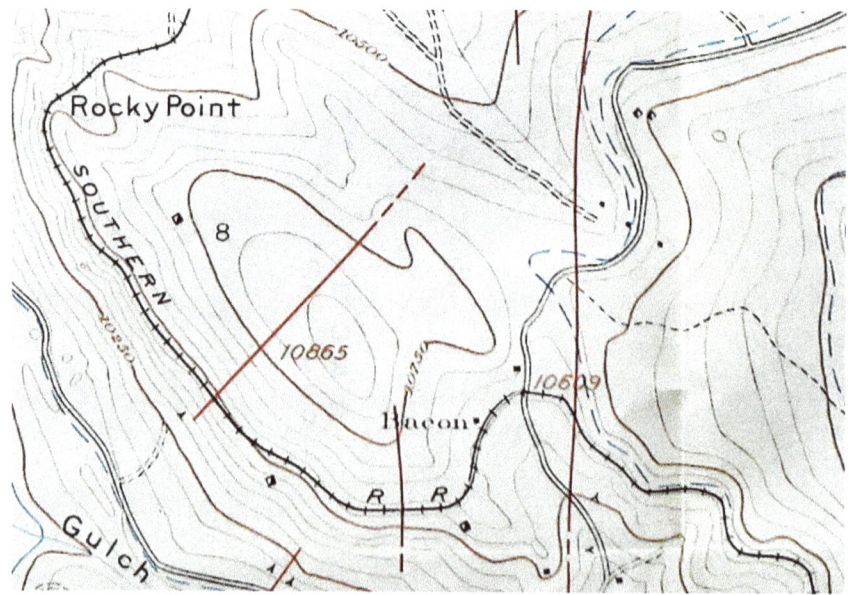

Figure 8-38. A Portion of a 1934 Map including Bacon. (T.S. Lovering, *Geology and Ore Deposits of the Breckenridge Mining District, Colorado*, Professional Paper 176, USGS)

Chapter 8 Argentine/Bacon Station

Abandonment

After years of lawsuits, the court permitted the Colorado & Southern to abandon the line in 1937 and remove the rails in 1938. **Figure 8-39** shows engine number 69 and the work crews removing trackage near Bacon station.

Figure 8-39. Engine No. 69 near Bacon Station, 1938. (Denver, South Park & Pacific Historical Society Collection)

Figure 8-40. Argentine/Bacon Site, 2021. Nothing remains except some pieces of glass in the meadow on the right. (Photograph by Author)

Figure 8-41. Aerial View of the Argentine/Bacon Site, 2021. The railroad tracks, with the spur to the left, follow today's Boreas Pass Road. (Google Earth, Imagery ©2021 Maxar Technologies, U.S. Geological Survey, USDA Farm Service Agency, Map data ©2021)

CHAPTER 9
ROCKY POINT

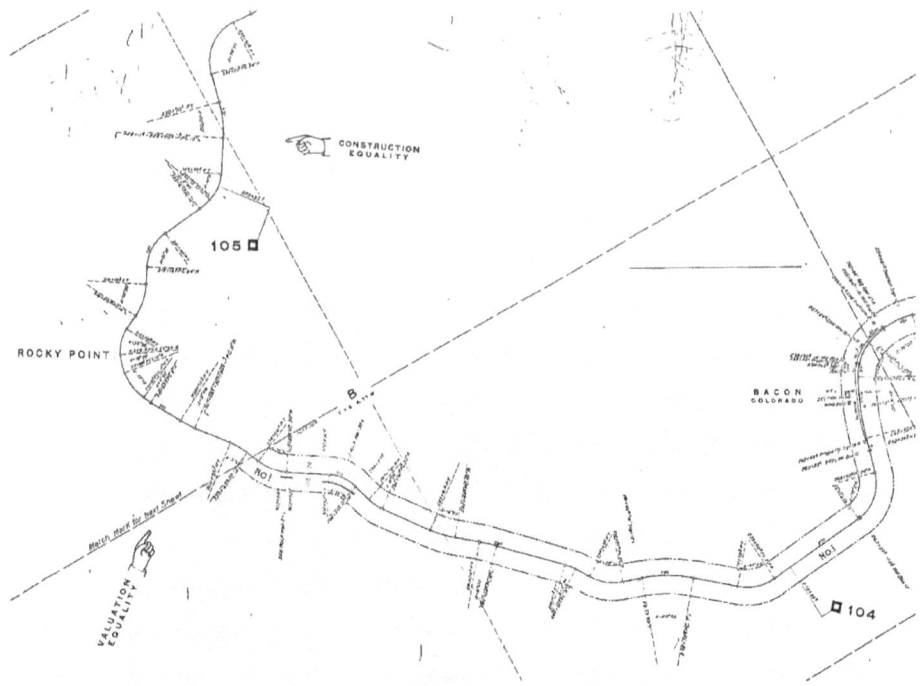

Figure 9-1. Portion of Colorado & Southern Map, 1918. The route went west from Bacon/Argentine, on the right, to the bend at Rocky Point. (Courtesy Bob Schoppe)

Site Location

Rocky Point does not fit the definition of a railroad station or spur. Instead, it became a favorite spot for the train to stop for passengers to disembark for a photograph or simply enjoy the view of Breckenridge and the Blue River valley.

The track, now Boreas Pass Road, cut through solid rock that today interests both professional and amateur geologists. The map in **Figure 9-1** shows the route as it went west from Bacon (Argentine), made the bend at Rocky Point, and then continued north to Breckenridge.

The newspapers highlighted the sometimes-pleasant experiences:
"A pleasant little picnic party left for Rocky Point on Thursday morning's train and returned on the train in the afternoon. They

were accompanied by O. Westerman, photographer, who took several views including a group of the merry picnickers." (**Figure 9-3**) (*Summit County Journal*, September 8, 1894)

"Photographer Westerman, on Sunday, took a number of fine 'view' pictures of the Ten-Mile mountains and the Blue river valley, as seen from the track of the Colorado & Southern, in the vicinity of Rocky Point." (*Summit County Journal*, October 28, 1899)

"Mr. T. E. Fisher, general passenger agent of the C. & S., has, for the tourist season of 1901, reissued that beautiful book, 'Picturesque Colorado,' showing many of the beauty spots along the South Park road. A number of the finer plates were made from photographs taken by O. Westerman. Rocky Point, Breckenridge, Nigger hill [renamed Barney Ford Hill], Uneva lake and the Ten-Mile, showing the Hotel Hamilton at Dillon, are among the prominent scenes in Summit county shown in that gem of the artist, author, printer and pressman." (*Summit County Journal*, June 1, 1901)

"On Saturday evening Marion Masden a brakeman, was thrown or fell from a train near Rocky point, near this city. Fortunately he was not seriously injured, but considerably jarred." (*Summit County Journal*, September 14, 1907)

"The geology class of the high school made a trip to Rocky Point yesterday. Miss Ward and Superintendent Bouton accompanied them, but the two latter rode back on the passenger train." (*Summit County Journal & Breckenridge Bulletin*, May 16, 1913)

"H. Heath, car inspector for the Colorado & Southern, had quite an exciting experience Thursday about noon. He hooked his push car on behind the morning passenger train and went up to Boreas to look after some work and this finished, was coasting down the hill on the car at a pretty fair clip. As he rounded Rocky Point a bunch of section men had just stepped off their hand car which they left on the track. Heath made a high dive and cleared the right-of-way. His car followed suit as it struck the other car and was badly smashed up. The hand car belonging to the section men did not leave the track but rounded all the mysterious curves nicely until it struck a freight train near the Gold Pan shops." *(Summit County Journal,* July 10, 1914)

"Members of the recently organized Boy Scouts patrols, celebrated Washington's birth-day anniversary by taking a hike to Rocky Point, under the leadership of Scoutmaster Gillmore. At midday they pitched camp and cooked and ate the true woodsmen style. They studied nature lore first-hand, discovered many interesting things about trees and rocks, trailed one another about just like the old-time scout when he had occasion to follow a trail, and returned home late in the afternoon, tired but elated. (*Summit County Journal,* February 26, 1916)

"As far as Summit County is concerned, the advertising literature recently issued by the Colorado and Southern is disappointing. As descriptive of the C. & S. system in general, the folder no doubt will prove effective, but Breckenridge is mentioned but once and only one illustration of this section appears—a familiar view of Rocky Point . . ." (*Summit County Journal,* June 3, 1916)

"The Scouts planned a hike to Rocky Point Saturday. During the meeting, which preceded the feed, much business of interest was taken up. A fine attendance gave impetus to the activities. Mr. Criswell was a visitor." (*Summit County Journal,* March 29, 1919)

Photographs from the mining era and the present show that Rocky Point still beckons visitors for a glimpse of the county's rich geologic and economic history. (**Figures 9-2** through **9-14**)

To the west, one sees the cirques of the glaciated crest of the Ten Mile Range and Mt. Quandary (elevation 14,265'). The sedimentary rocks on either side of the road/former railroad right-of-way tell a story that started

Chapter 9 Rocky Point

many millions of years ago when a shallow inland sea covered the area. As the depth of water in the shallow sea changed, sediments created thinly bedded shale in deeper water and more thickly bedded sandstone in shallow, beach environments. The two types of rock weather differently; the shale more quickly than the sandstone. Crustal compression lifted the layers over 9,000 feet, turned them 90 degrees as they rose, and created cracks into which light-colored granitic dikes intruded. (**Figure 9-12**) High on the rock wall facing north on the east side of the roadbed, sharp eyes will see ripple marks created in the shallow water of the ancient beach environment.

Figure 9-2. Train with Helper Engine at Rocky Point heading toward Boreas Pass. (Courtesy Maureen Nicholls)

Figure 9-3. Enjoying a Picnic at Rocky Point. Otto Westerman photographed the group on September 6, 1894. They arrived on the morning train and returned to Breckenridge on the afternoon train. (Courtesy Maureen Nicholls)

Figure 9-4. Trailer at Rocky Point. Using these self-powered conveyances, variously called a motorcar, speeder, popcar or putt-putt, maintenance crews rode the rails checking for problems. This group of men, obviously not railroad workers, posed for a picture on their trailer. In the background, workers have stockpiled replacement ties. (Courtesy Denver, South Park & Pacific Historical Society)

Chapter 9 Rocky Point

Figure 9-5. Engine No. 113. Built in 1884, No. 113 hauled freight and passengers until 1938. The train crew and an executive stopped for a photograph. (Courtesy Maureen Nicholls)

Figure 9-6. A Special Young Lady. Engine No. 205 paused at Rocky Point to allow Clinton H Scott to photograph the young lady sitting on the pilot of the locomotive. (Courtesy Ed and Nanacy Bathke)

Chapter 9 Rocky Point

Figure 9-7. Checking the Track at Rocky Point. Trackmen regularly checked the track for any problems. Note the lack of ballast to the outside of the rails and the supply of replacement ties. (Courtesy Ed and Nancy Bathke)

Figure 9-8. Mixed Train stopping at Rocky Point. Passengers have disembarked for a photograph. (Courtesy Maureen Nicholls)

Figure 9-9. A Dangerous Climb. Climbing the unconsolidated sedimentary rocks presented danger, especially to women in long skirts. (Courtesy Maureen Nicholls)

Figure 9-10. Rocky Point, 1970. The layered sandstone and shale, prominent at Rocky Point, have been intruded by a light-colored granitic dike, one of many in the area. (Courtesy Maureen Nicholls)

Figure 9-11. Approaching Rocky Point from Breckenridge, 2022. High on the rock face are ripple marks created by a shallow inland sea that overed the area millions of years ago. (Photograph by Author)

Figure 9-12. Boreas Pass Road passes between Sheer Rock Faces, 2022. Compare to Figures 9-4 and 9-7. (Photograph by Author)

Figure 9-13. Approaching Rocky Point from Boreas Pass, 2022. Compare to Figures 9-6 and 9-9. (Photograph by Author)

Figure 9-14. Northeast of Rocky Point. Compare to Figures 9-2 and 9-5. (Photograph by Author)

BIBLIOGRAPHY

Books, Articles, and Mining District Logs

Crofutt, George A. *Grip Sack Guide to Colorado*. Overland Publishing Company, 1881.

Crofutt, George A. *Grip Sack Guide to Colorado*. Overland Publishing Company, 1885.

Daugherty, John. *Cultural Resource Inventories for Summit County, Colorado, Part II, Survey of Historic Mines and Mining Camps – Swan River and French Creek*. Summit Historical Society, 1974.

Lovering, T.S. *Geology and Ore Deposits of the Breckenridge Mining District, Colorado*, Professional Paper 176, U.S. Geological Survey. Washington, D.C.: Government Printing Office, 1934.

Poor, M.C. *Denver South Park & Pacific*. World Press, 1949.

Kindig, R.H.; Haley, E.J.; Poor, M.C. Pictorial Supplement to *Denver South Park & Pacific*. World Press, 1959.

Ransome, Frederick Leslie. *Geology and Ore Deposits of the Breckenridge District, Colorado*. Professional Paper 75, Department of the Interior, U.S. Geological Survey. Washington, D.C.: Government Printing Office, 1911.

Schoppe, Bob & Mather, Sandra F. Pritchard. *Summit County's Narrow-Gauge Railroads*. Arcadia Publishing, 2016.

Singewald, Quentin D. *Geology and Ore Deposits of the Upper Blue River Area, Summit County, Colorado*, Geological Survey Bulletin 970. United States Government Printing Office, Washington, D.C.: 1951.

Bibliography

Newspapers and Magazines

1. The website, Colorado Historic Newspapers Collection at https://www.coloradohistoricnewspapers.org

    a. *Summit County Journal*, 1891 to 1909 and 1914 to 1923, Breckenridge, Colorado
    b. *Breckenridge Bulletin*, 1899 to 1909, Breckenridge, Colorado
    c. *Summit County Journal and Breckenridge Bulletin*, 1909 to 1914, Breckenridge, Colorado
    d. Miscellaneous other historic Colorado newspapers

2. *Colorado Postal Historian*, Volume 16, Number 1, August, 2000

Other Sources

Bureau of Land Management, Lakewood, Colorado

Colorado School of Mines, Arthur Lakes Library, Golden, Colorado

Colorado State Archives, Denver, Colorado

Denver Public Library, Western History Section, Denver, Colorado

Breckenridge History Archives, Breckenridge, Colorado

History Colorado, Denver, Colorado

Summit County Clerk and Recorder's Office, Breckenridge, Colorado

Summit Historical Society Archives, Dillon, Colorado

INDEX

7-30 Mine: 80, 90-92, 95, 97-102
Aco Mining and Leasing Company: 192
Alpha Mines Company: 92
Balsome and Handy Lodes (MS9579): 114-116, 118-120, 122
Blue Flag Mining & Milling Company: 180-183, 188
Christensen, Fred: 148
Como: 10, 12, 14, 15, 18-22, 25, 28, 30, 31, 33, 34, 53, 54, 59, 64, 78, 134, 202, 204, 205, 218
Consolidated Mining Company: 79, 92
Dickey: 11, 14, 18, 24, 29, 65
Dillon: 8-12, 28, 29, 31, 39, 42, 64, 134, 182, 213
Dillon, Sydney: 42, 46
Engine No. 9: 67
Engine House: 43-46, 53, 55, 56, 60, 62, 68, 73
Farnham, William H.: 76, 78, 79
Finding, C.A.: 148, 149, 151
Foote, Harry C.: 137, 138, 141, 147
Foote, Robert: 148, 150
Goodhue, John: 14
Great Blockade/Big Snow: 18-20, 58-64, 134, 139, 140
Hill, James J.: 30
Hostettler, Joseph J.: 90, 91
Iliff, William H.: 91
Laurium Gold Consolidated Company: 184, 188
Laurium Lode (MS2673): 177, 178
Laurium Mine & Mill: 176-200
Laurium Mining Company: 179
McBarnes Mining District: 78, 113, 114
McKillip, R.C.: 148
Motorcar: 216
Mountain Pride Gold Mining Company: 136, 137, 141, 146, 149, 151
Mountain Pride Mine & Mill: 136-141, 142, 144-163
Palmer, William Jackson: 8
Pike, Calvin H.: 78-80, 92
Popcar: 216

Post Office: 57, 58, 76, 78-80, 176
Putt-putt: 216
Robinson, George: 33, 92, 96, 97, 188
Rotary Snowplow: 15-20, 25, 27, 40, 63, 64, 115, 134, 139, 166, 203-206
Roundhouse: 53, 54
Schwartz, Oswald B.: 22, 23
Seven-Thirty Lode (MS5578): 90
Silver Queen Lode (MS2222): 90, 91
Snow Blockade/Big Snow: 18-20, 58-64, 134, 139, 140
Snowshed: 29, 30, 55, 59, 67
South Park Zephyr: 93-96
Speeder: 117, 216
Sunny Side Lode (MS9580): 113-116
Ten Mile Canyon: 8, 10, 11, 25-27, 31, 65
West Laurium Lode (MS2674): 178, 182
Williams, Dan: 65, 66
Wood, Wilber F.: 78-80

ABOUT THE AUTHORS

Bill Fountain

Bill Fountain grew up in Southern California where he began working in the tire business while still in high school and eventually became part-owner of 23 Big O Tires stores. He and his wife, Jeanne, moved to Denver in 1987 when he was a vice-president of Big O Tires, Inc. In 1988, he purchased several of the Big O Tires stores in the Denver metro area. Although he sold his last three tire stores in December, 2009, Bill still does some consulting for other Big O Tires dealers.

In 1988, after he and Jeanne purchased a home in Breckenridge, Bill began spending his summers investigating old cabins, mines, and ghost towns and collecting books and photos. He teams with Rich Skovlin, Maureen Nicholls, and Rick Hague exploring backcountry sites. Bill spent many hours looking through records in the Summit County Courthouse in Breckenridge; Breckenridge History Archives; the Bureau of Land Management Archives in Lakewood; the Federal Center in Lakewood; the Colorado School of Mines, Arthur Lakes Library in Golden; History Colorado; and the Denver Public Library—as well as reading historic newspapers on the Colorado Historic Newspapers website. He has transcribed over 3,500 pages of Breckenridge mining history and has a collection of more than 3,500 digitized photographs from the 1860s to 1980s. During the summer months, Bill gives special presentations and leads tours for the Summit Historical Society, Breckenridge History (previously Breckenridge Heritage Alliance), and the Frisco Historic Park & Museum.

Bill and Jeanne traveled to Hawaii in 1969 on their honeymoon spending time in Honolulu, Kauai, and in Kailua Kona on the Big Island. They returned several times to Kona in the 1970s and 1980s. In 1994, they purchased a time share at Kona Coast Resort, spending five weeks there each year. In 2003, they purchased a small condo; and in 2005, they upgraded to a large townhouse. In January, 2010, now fully retired, they purchased a home where they spend eight to nine months a year.

Even while in Hawaii, Bill continues his research on Breckenridge history. He and Jeanne return to their home in Highlands Ranch for the summers to be near their children and grandchildren. They rent a place in Summit County for two months each summer as Bill continues exploring the fascinating history of Summit County.

Bill has worked on special research projects for local authors, Mary Ellen Gilliland and Dr. Sandra Mather, Breckenridge History, Summit Historical Society, and the Breckenridge History Archives.

In 2014, Bill received the prestigious Theobald Award from Breckenridge History for his contributions to the preservation of Breckenridge's history.

In 2023, Bill received a lifetime membership to the Summit Historical Society.

Dr. Sandra F. Pritchard Mather

Dr. Sandra F. Pritchard Mather is a *professor emerita* in the Department of Earth and Space Sciences at West Chester University in Pennsylvania where she taught geology and meteorology before retiring in May, 1999. Since coming to Summit County in 1980 to complete her doctoral dissertation for the University of Oregon, she has written many books about the geologic, geographic, and historic landscapes of the county and those who lived here from 1859 until the turn of the century: *Southern Summit, A Geographer's Perspective; Roadside Summit, Part I, the Natural Landscape; Roadside Summit, Part II, the Human Landscape; Dillon, Denver, and the Dam; Men, Mining, and Machines; Behind Swinging Doors, the Saloons of Breckenridge and Summit County, Colorado—1859 to 1900; Golden Gulches, Hydraulic Mining in and around Breckenridge, Colorado; Summit County*, part of the Arcadia Images of America series; *Frisco and the Ten Mile Canyon*, also part of the Arcadia Images of America series; *They weren't all Prostitutes and Gamblers, the Women of Summit County from 1859 to the Turn of the Century; Historic Footprints, A Picture Book for Young Readers*; with Rick Hague, *Windows to the Past*, and with Bob Schoppe, the *Narrow-Gauge Railroads of Summit County*, part of the Arcadia Images of Rail series. Sandie is co-author with Bill Fountain of the *Chasing the Dream* series, *Chasing the Bad Guys, Enforcing the Law in Breckenridge, Colorado, Town Marshals 1881-1923*, and *Country Boy Mine, Breckenridge, Colorado, 1881-1994*.

Sandie spent summers in Summit County leading tours and presenting special programs for the Summit Historical Society, the Frisco Historic Park & Museum, and Breckenridge History. In 2013, Sandie received the prestigious Theobald Award from Breckenridge History for her contributions to the preservation of Breckenridge's history. She is a former president and life member of the Summit Historical Society.

www.ingramcontent.com/pod-product-compliance
Lightning Source LLC
Chambersburg PA
CBHW050141170426
43197CB00011B/1923